Ivan Moscovich's
MASTERMIND COLLECTION

The Hinged Square & Other Puzzles

STERLING PUBLISHING CO., INC.
New York

To Anitta, Hila, and Emilia, with love

Ivan Moscovich Mastermind Collection:
The Hinged Square & Other Puzzles was edited, designed, and typset by Imagine Puzzles Ltd.,
London (info@imaginepuzzles.com)

EDITORIAL DIRECTOR
Alison Moore
ASSISTANT EDITOR
David Popey
ART EDITOR
Keith Miller
CONSULTANT EDITOR
David Bodycombe
PROJECT MANAGER
Tamiko Rex
PUBLISHING DIRECTOR
Hal Robinson

Clipart: Nova Development Corporation

Library of Congress Cataloging-in-Publication Data Available

2 4 6 8 10 9 7 5 3 1

Published by Sterling Publishing Co., Inc.
387 Park Avenue South, New York, NY 10016
© 2004 by Ivan Moscovich
Distributed in Canada by Sterling Publishing
c/o Canadian Manda Group, 165 Dufferin Street,
Toronto, Ontario, Canada M6K 3H6
Distributed in Great Britain by Chrysalis Books Group PLC
The Chrysalis Building, Bramley Road, London W10 6SP, England
Distributed in Australia by Capricorn Link (Australia) Pty. Ltd.
P.O. Box 704, Windsor, NSW 2756, Australia

Sterling ISBN 1-4027-1666-4

Contents

Introduction

Ever since my high school days I have loved puzzles and mathematical recreational problems. This love developed into a hobby when, by chance, some time in 1956, I encountered the first issue of *Scientific American* with Martin Gardner's mathematical games column. And for the past 50 years or so I have been designing and inventing teaching aids, puzzles, games, toys, and hands-on science museum exhibits.

Recreational mathematics is mathematics with the emphasis on fun, but, of course, this definition is far too general. The popular fun and pedagogic aspects of recreational mathematics overlap considerably, and there is no clear boundary between recreational and "serious" mathematics. You don't have to be a mathematician to enjoy mathematics. It is just another language, the language of creative thinking and problem-solving, which will enrich your life, like it did and still does mine.

Many people seem convinced that it is possible to get along quite nicely without any mathematical knowledge. This is not so: Mathematics is the basis of all knowledge and the bearer of all high culture. It is never too late to start enjoying and learning the basics of math, which will furnish our all-too sluggish brains with solid mental exercise and provide us with a variety of pleasures to which we may be entirely unaccustomed.

In collecting and creating puzzles, I favor those that are more than just fun, preferring instead puzzles that offer opportunities for intellectual satisfaction and learning experiences, as well as provoking curiosity and creative thinking. To stress these criteria, I call my puzzles Thinkthings.

The *Mastermind Collection* series systematically covers a wide range of mathematical ideas, through a great variety of puzzles, games, problems, and much more, from the best classical puzzles taken from the history of mathematics to many entirely original ideas.

This book, *The Hinged Square & Other Puzzles*, contains Henry Dudeney's classic square-to-triangle transformation, one of the real gems of recreational mathematics, and leads on to a vast array of classic and novel puzzles, games, and more.

A great effort has been made to make all the puzzles understandable to everybody, though some of the solutions may be hard work. For this reason, the ideas are presented in a novel and highly esthetic visual form, making it easier to perceive the underlying mathematics.

More than ever before, I hope that these books will convey my enthusiasm for and fascination with mathematics and share these with the reader. They combine fun and entertainment with intellectual challenges, through which a great number of ideas, basic concepts common to art, science, and everyday life, can be enjoyed and understood.

Some of the games included are designed so that they can easily be made and played. The structure of many is such that they will excite the mind, suggest new ideas and insights, and pave the way for new modes of thought and creative expression.

Despite the diversity of topics, there is an underlying continuity in the topics included. Each individual Thinkthing can stand alone (even if it is, in fact, related to many others), so you can dip in at will without the frustration of cross-referencing.

I hope you will enjoy the *Mastermind Collection* series and Thinkthings as much as I have enjoyed creating them for you.

—Ivan Moscovich

If you're having a bad day, sit down, put your feet up, and take revenge on the innocent squares and circles on these pages. They are ripe for being sliced and divided in interesting ways.

▼ THE HINGED SQUARE

The hinged square transformation of Henry Ernest Dudeney is a real gem of recreational geometry. He dissected a square into four parts. Hinges, marked here in black, connect the parts to each other. If you leave the blue piece fixed and swing the others around their hinges, you can rearrange the pieces to form a new shape. Just by looking, can you guess what the new shape will be?

ANSWER: PAGE 98

Geometric dissection

What is a geometric dissection? This is when a geometric figure is cut into pieces that can be rearranged to form another, new figure.

The goal of the great puzzle inventors Sam Loyd and Henry Dudeney was to minimize the number of pieces from which such transformations can be obtained. In doing so they created many mathematical puzzles that have enjoyed great popularity ever since.

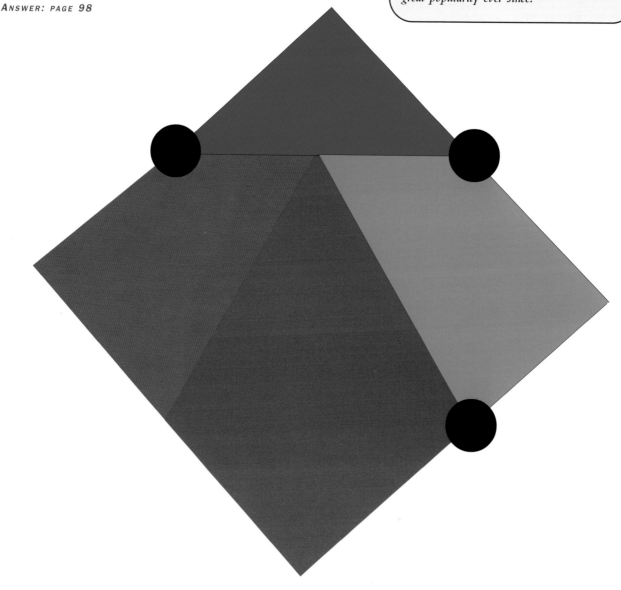

▼ MIQUEL'S THEOREM

We have drawn a circle and marked four points on it: A, B, C, and D. Then circles were drawn through A and B, B and C, C and D, and D and A. The four intersections of these four circles also lie on a circle, as shown. Will this always be the case? Try it and find out.

ANSWER: PAGE 98

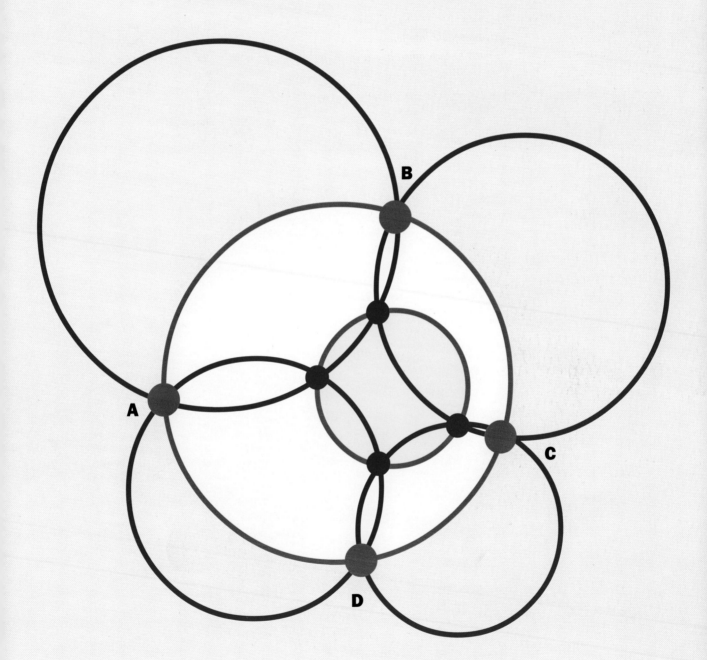

We all take points and lines for granted. But points are not just marks—they are mathematical symbols that define position. And lines are not only the fundamental elements of drawn images but also mathematical symbols that link points, indicate distance and direction, and define space. Points and lines—and the relationships between them—are the basic tools of geometry. The ancient Greeks had to turn geometry from the practical study of measuring land to the science of abstract form before they could produce mathematical proofs.

EUCLID OF ALEXANDRIA (325–265 B.C.)

Euclid of Alexandria is one of the most famous mathematicians of antiquity. He is best known for his books on mathematics, The Elements, *the greatest mathematical textbooks of all time. Euclid was the leader of a team of mathematicians, all of whom contributed to the work that has since become known as his.*

He is also regarded as the greatest mathematics teacher ever. Despite that, little reliable information has been found about his life.

Consisting of 13 books, The Elements *was a compilation of knowledge on mathematics that became the basis of mathematics teaching for 2,000 years. Euclid's* Elements *is also remarkable for the clarity with which the theorems are stated and proved.*

✳ Basic tools of geometry

The Greeks introduced problems that required figures to be constructed by the use of a straightedge and compass alone. Three famous problems left by the ancient Greeks have resisted the efforts of many mathematicians over the centuries to solve them: duplicating the cube (constructing a cube double the volume of a given cube, 1); squaring the circle (constructing a square equal in area to a given circle, 2); and trisecting the angle (dividing a given angle into three equal parts, 3). None of these problems is solvable using only a compass and unmarked straightedge, or even at all.

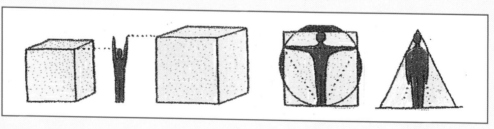

1　　　　　　　　　　**2**　　　**3**

❉ Drawing regular polygons with a compass

One of the the most beautiful problems of antiquity is that of constructing regular polygons. The ancient Greeks set up a challenging set of game rules in relation to geometry. They restricted the tools to be used for creating geometrical figures to a compass and straightedge only. The first theorem in Euclid's *Elements* was the construction of the equilateral triangle. The noted German artist Albrecht Dürer was an expert at drawing exact geometrical figures by this method.

Can you follow Dürer and construct the figures shown on the following pages using a compass and straightedge only? Measuring of distances and angles is not allowed. Dürer's techniques are demonstrated on each page.

Emperor Napoleon, intrigued by these problems, posed some new variations, as did Lorenzo Mascheroni (1750–1800), an Italian mathematician who proved that every figure which can be constructed by compass and straightedge can be constructed by compass alone.

In 1795, 19-year-old Carl Friedrich Gauss proved which polygons can be constructed by compass and straight-edge and which can't, quite a difficult problem. His first great achievement was the construction of the regular 17-gon. It was chronicled that young Gauss was so pleased by his discovery that he chose mathematics as his profession.

So a seemingly simple problem became a whole series of problems. For some values of "n" (number of sides of the polygon) it is a very simple problem; for some other values it is a bit more difficult, but there are values of n for which the problem is extremely difficult (such as the n = 17 problem of Gauss). And, finally, there are values of n for which the problem cannot be solved at all. The red numbers below indicate the values for n for which regular polygons can be constructed; those in black show the ones that cannot.

There is a law that defines whether a given number should be black or red, but it is quite difficult to describe without resorting to number theory, the most advanced area of arithmetic.

3, 4, 5, 6, 7, 8, 9, 10, 11, 12, 13, 14, 15, 16, 17, 18, 19, 20, 21, 22, 23, 24, 25, 26, 27, 28, 29, 30, 31, 32, 33, 34, 35, 36, 37, 38, 39, 40, 41, 42, 43, 44, 45, 46, 47, 48, ...

Creating polygons using only a compass and straight-edge is a very logical and satisfying geometrical activity. The ancient Greeks, and many others later, such as the German artist Albrecht Dürer, created the groundwork of geometry in this way. Dürer's techniques are demonstrated on the pages that follow. Can you draw the given shapes on the following pages? Remember: You can use a compass and a straightedge only, and no measuring of distances or angles is allowed.

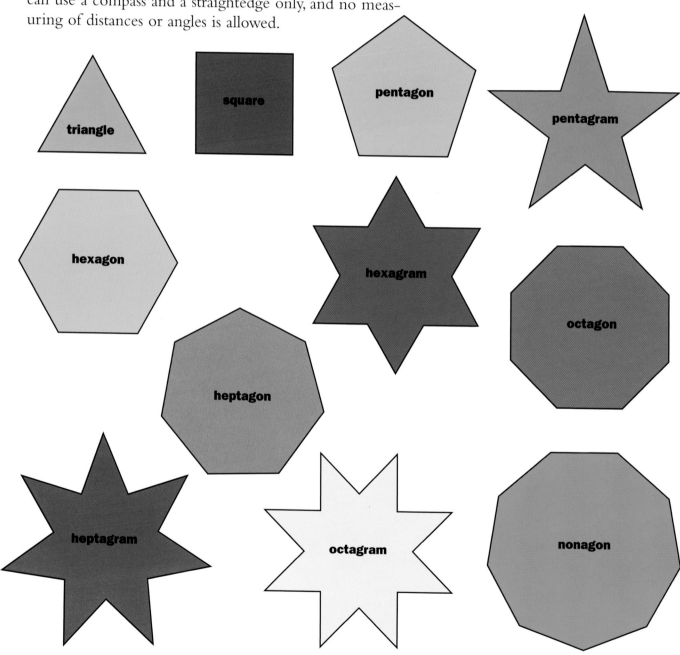

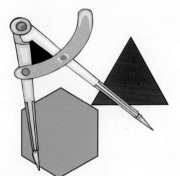

◀ DRAWING A TRIANGLE AND A HEXAGON

The challenge here is to draw an equilateral triangle and a regular hexagon.

How to do it:

Place the compass point on the black dot and draw a circle of any size you like. Without changing the compass setting, place the needle of the compass somewhere on the circle and draw a new circle. Where your new circle intersects the original, draw another circle. Repeat four more times, then number the intersection points as shown at right. To reveal the equilateral triangle, connect with straight lines points **1–3**, **3–5**, and **5–1**. For the hexagon connect with straight lines points **1–2**, **2–3**, **3–4**, **4–5**, **5–6**, and **6–1**.

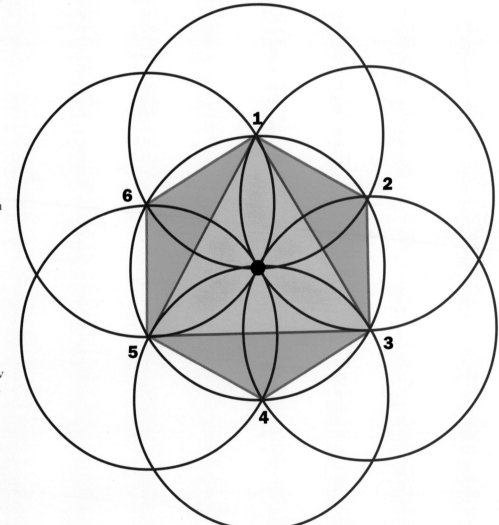

▶ DRAWING A SQUARE

This time, can you draw a perfect square? It may not be as easy as it sounds…

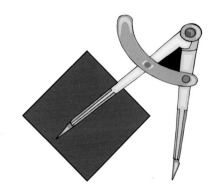

How to do it:

Place the compass point on the black dot and draw a circle, again of any size you like. Draw a horizontal line through the black center, and where it cuts the circle, mark **1** and **2**. Widen the jaws of the compasses and place its point at 1 and mark off an arc above the circle. Without changing the setting, repeat this at **2** to get point **3**. Draw a vertical line through the center point of the circle from **3** to the bottom of the circle to get points **4** and **5**. Draw straight lines connecting points **1–4**, **4–2**, **2–5**, and **5–1** to create a perfect square in the circle.

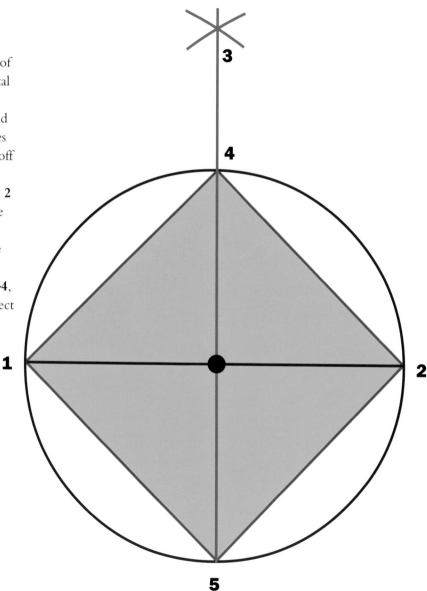

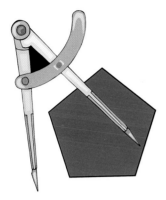

◀ **DRAWING A REGULAR PENTAGON**
*Still following the rules on page 9, can you
draw a regular five-sided pentagon, like the one
shown on the left?*

How to do it:

The regular pentagon can be
constructed without changing the
compass setting. Draw two circles
(shown here in blue) so that they
pass through each other's centers.
Now draw a line between the two
center points **a** and **b**. This is the
base of the regular pentagon.

Where the two circles cross, mark
c on the top and **d** on the bottom.
Draw a straight line from **d–c** and
extend it upward. Place the point of
the compass on **d** and draw another
circle (shown in red) through the
two circles at their centers **a** and **b**.

Where the third circle cuts the
other two circles, mark **e** and **f**.
Where the vertical line **c–d** is
crossed, mark **g**. Now draw a
straight line between **e** and **g** and
extend it to the far edge of the
circle, marking this point as **h**. Draw
another straight line between **f** and
g and extend it to the circle,
marking this point **i**. Connect **i** with
a, and **h** with **b** and you will have
two more sides of the regular
pentagon. With the point of the
compass on **i** mark off **j** on the
extended **d–c** line. Join **i** to **j** and **h**
to **j** to complete the pentagon.

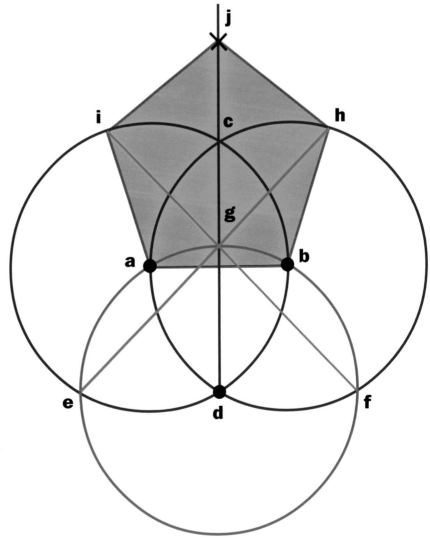

Here's a bit of light relief—from drawing shapes to seeing shapes within shapes. The aim here is to discover regular and compound polygons within the range of shapes below. Look carefully—you'll be surprised how many you can find.

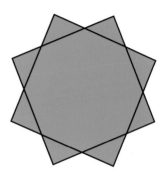

Regular octagon **Regular octagonal star** **Regular compound octagon of two squares**

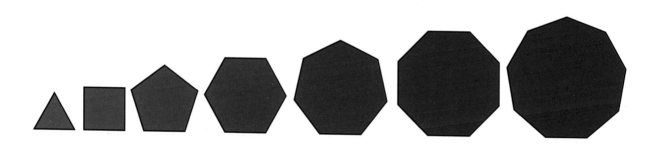

▲ REGULAR POLYGONS AND STARS

A polygon is called regular if it has the following two properties:

1. All its sides are equal.

2. All its angles are equal.

   A circle may be thought of as a regular polygon with an infinite number of sides. There are also an infinite number of regular polygons that can be subdivided into the following subgroups, demonstrated by a regular octagon:

1. Simple regular polygons.

2. Regular star polygons.

3. Regular compound polygons.

   How many regular star and compound polygons are there, starting from an equilateral triangle, and up to to a regular nonagon?

ANSWER: PAGE 98

◄ DRAWING A HEXAGRAM

*Can you find a way to draw
a hexagram, a six-pointed star?*

How to do it:

The six-pointed star is very similar to the triangle/hexagon construction we met on page 11. We've replicated the main triangular part of the diagram on the right (using letters instead of numbers).

Note that if you draw two overlapping equilateral triangles, you will arrive at a hexagram. One triangle joins points **b**, **d**, and **f**. The other triangle joins **g**, **c**, and **e**. That's all there is to it!

▶ DRAWING A REGULAR HEPTAGON

Have a think about this one. Can you draw a regular heptagon, a figure with seven sides?

How to do it:
Place the compass point on the black dot and draw a circle of any size you like. Construct an equilateral triangle using the method shown on page 11.

Draw a straight line from **2** through the center to the side of the triangle and mark this point as **b**. Set the compass to the distance between number **1** and **b** and mark off the point on the circle **c**. Place the point of the compass on **c** and mark off **d**, then continue to mark points **e**, **f**, **g**, and **h**. Join these points to get the heptagon.

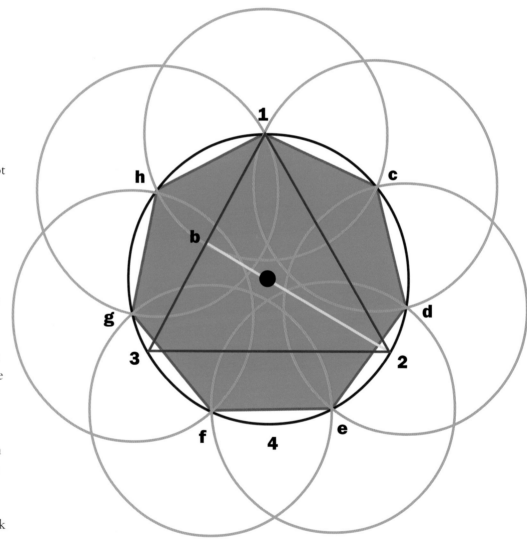

◀ **DRAWING A REGULAR HEPTAGRAM**
A heptagram is a septagonal star (one with seven sides). Can you draw one following the rules listed on page 9?

How to do it:

Follow the instructions to make a heptagon set out on page 16. Set the compass at approximately half the radius of the circle and with the point at **a** draw a circle (shown in yellow).

With the compass needle at number **1** and then **c**, mark off arcs outside the circle and draw a line from where the arcs intersect at **4** to **a**. Mark where this line crosses the circle as **i**.

Reset the compass between number **1** and **i**. Place the point of the compass on **c** and mark off **j**. Continue in this way, marking off round the whole circle.

Starting at **a**, draw lines to **j**, **k**, **l**, **m**, **n**, and **o**. From where these lines cut the inner circle, draw lines to number **1**, **c**, **d**, **e**, **f**, **g**, and **h** to make the points of the star.

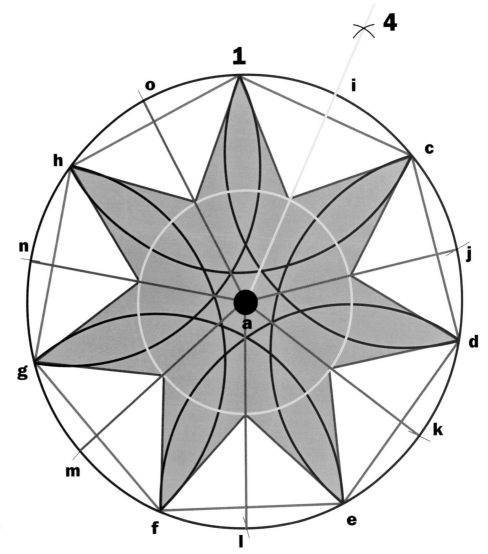

▶ DRAWING A REGULAR OCTAGON

Can you figure out an octagon? Its eight sides may prove tricky.

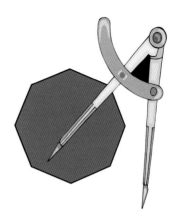

How to do it:

First, construct a square as on page 12.

Draw two circles that are slightly smaller than the original, centered at **1** and **4**. These will cross at point **a**. From **a**, draw a line to the center to get point **6**. Reset the compass between **1** and **6** and mark off the other halfway points on the sides of the square. Draw lines between all eight points to produce a regular octagon.

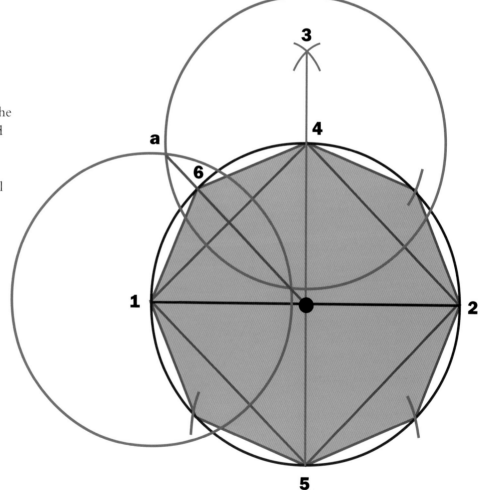

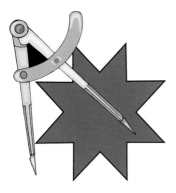

◄ DRAWING AN OCTAGRAM

From octagon to octagram, an eight-sided star like the one on the left. Can you work out how to draw one?

How to do it:

Follow the instructions to make an octagon given on page 18. This will identify eight points around the circle.

Start at any point. Now count three points around the circumference (for instance, if you start at point 1, your first destination point will be point 4). Next, draw a straight line between these points.

Count three more positions around the circle (from point 4 to point 7, then to point 2, and so on), always moving in the same direction. Draw a line between those two points and keep going until you have visited all eight points.

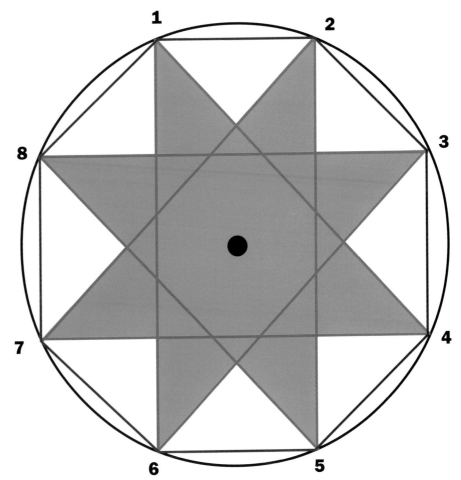

▶ DRAWING A REGULAR NONAGON

Our last challenge in this section is to draw a regular nonagon. Its nine sides require a good mind and a steady hand.

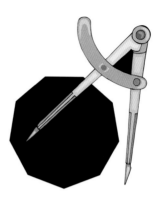

How to do it:

First draw a vertical line and mark its lower end **a**. Set the compass about two-thirds up the line from **a** and mark the point **2**. Divide the line **a–2** by marking off arcs to to the left and right with the point of the compass at **a** and then **2**. Where the arcs intersect, mark as **3** and **4**. Draw a line between **3** and **4** and where it crosses the vertical line mark as number **1**. Set the compass between **a** and **1**.

Move the compass point to **2** and mark off the upper vertical line at **b**. Set the compass between **a** and **b** and draw a circle. Without changing the compass setting, place the pencil on **b**, the point on the circle to the right at **y**, and draw an arc inside. Mark **c** where the arc meets the circle. Place the compass pencil on **b** and the point on the circle to the left at **x** and draw an arc inside. Mark **d** where the arc meets the circle.

Where the **3–1–4** line crosses the arcs **b–a–c** and **b–a–d**, mark **e** and **f**. Set the compass between **a** and **e** and draw a circle. Reset the compass between **e** and **f** and mark off nine equal parts of the circle. Join these to create the nonagon.

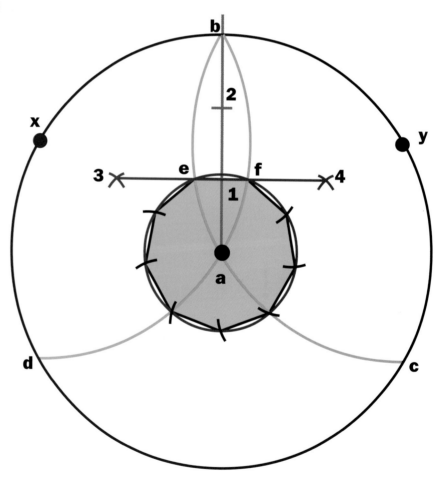

▲ **CIRCLE LOTTO**

Just by looking can you decipher this good advice?

ANSWER: PAGE 99

Did you know that honeybees were once thought to be color blind? The German scientist Dr. Karl von Frisch proved, however, that bees actually have three-color vision similar to ours. This he demonstrated by training them to detect blue sugar-coated squares in a grid of plain gray squares.

Queen bee

◄ BEELINE TO THE QUEEN

The bee society is the world's most efficiently run organization.

So it is no wonder that the billboard at the entrance to their honeycomb colony provides the bees with enough information to work out the exact layout and location of the queen bee's cell.

Can you pinpoint it?

ANSWER: PAGE 99

▼ **PEGBOARD SQUARES**

How many different sizes of squares can you get by stretching a rubber band along four pegs of the pegboard?

ANSWER: PAGE 100

Many three-dimensional shapes can be formed by taking a simple two-dimensional shape and rotating it in some way. For example, rotating a disc about its diameter would form a sphere, and rotating a line about a parallel line would give a cylinder. Such shapes are termed "surfaces of revolution." Have a go at this one.

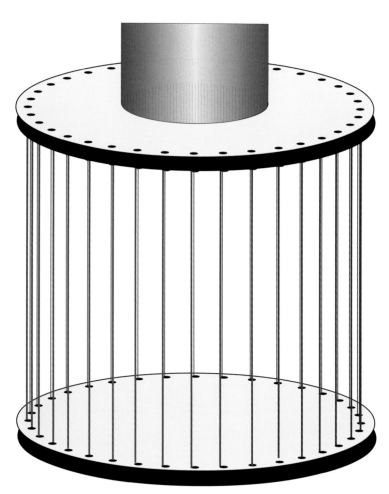

◀ TRANSFORMABLE CYLINDER

The upper disk of this transformable cylinder is fixed to the ceiling, while the lower disk is freely suspended on stretched rubber bands. What will be the configuration of the structure when the lower disk is rotated 90 degrees clockwise or counterclockwise 180 degrees? Can families of straight lines create curved surfaces?

ANSWER: PAGE **100**

✳ Hyperbolas and hyperboloids

The hyperboloid is an example of a ruled surface where a three-dimensional curved surface has been created from one-dimensional straight lines. It is based on the hyperbola, a type of curve that is frequently found in the study of ballistics and in the path of some comets. In fact, if you look at the sides of the hyperboloid you can see the two-dimensional hyperbola curve.

The hyperbola is a very useful shape. For a good example, look at satellite dishes. That these are based on the hyperbola is no coincidence. No matter which part of the dish the TV signal hits, it will be focused to the same point, thus improving the strength of the signal.

▲ STAINED GLASS WINDOW

Some tiles are missing. What color should they be?

ANSWER: PAGE 100

It was a bad day at the train factory. As you may know from the wheels of steam trains, connector rods are used to change circular motion into sideways motion. As an experiment, the factory has made a few different sets of wheels with a connector rod between them, but unfortunately someone forgot to label the results of their experiment. Can you help them out?

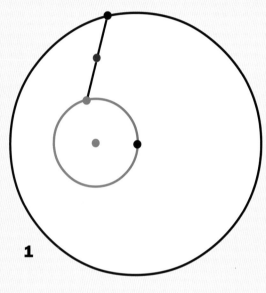

1

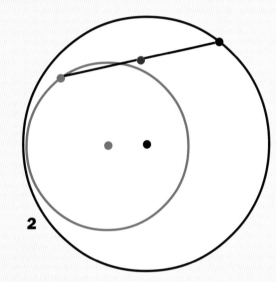

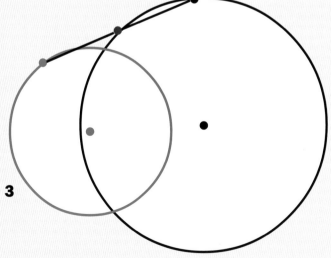

2

3

▶ COUPLING UP

Imagine that the black line is a rod connected at either end to two wheels (the green and blue circles). The green wheel rotates causing the rod to move and the other end (on the blue circle) to slide around appropriately.

If you were to draw a path showing the movement of the middle of the black line, represented by the red dot, what would you trace? Match up the wheel systems (1 to 5) with the paths given (A to E).

ANSWER: PAGE 101

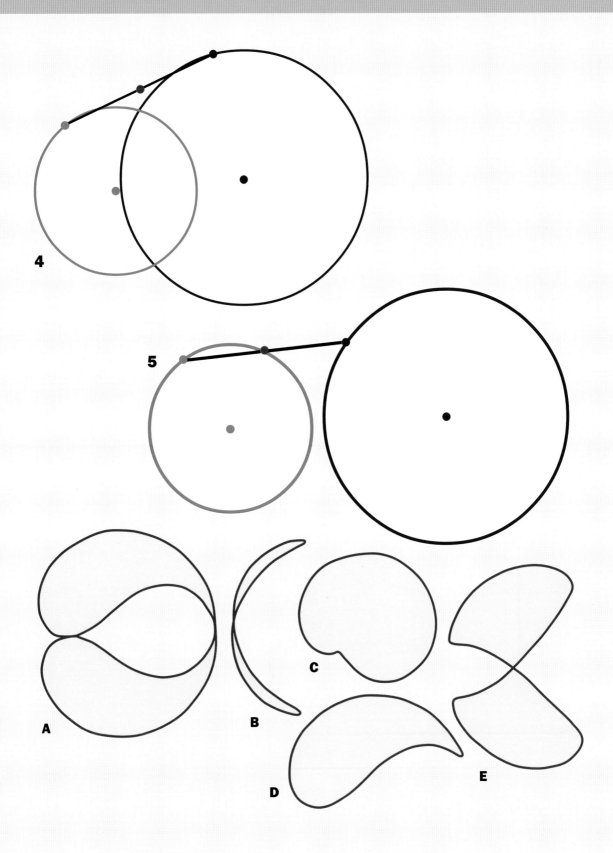

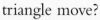

The next day, the train company tried out another experiment. This time, they connected the wheels with a triangle and fixed two points of its corners to the wheel. How, they wondered, would the free point of the triangle move?

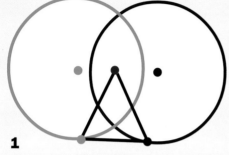

1

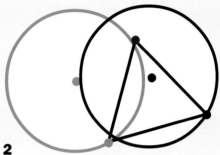

2

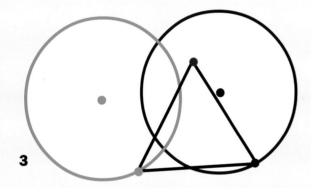

3

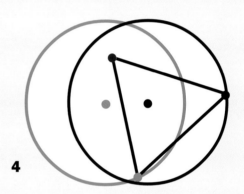

4

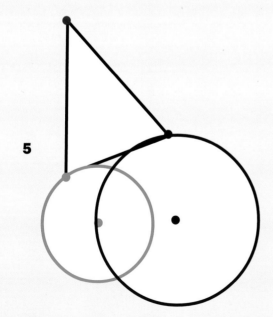

5

◀ **TRIANGULAR TRANSPORTERS**

Imagine a triangle linkage (1–5), with its two endpoints constrained to two circles. Can you puzzle out the paths traced by the third point of the five triangles as the triangles move through a full circle and so identify which curve (A–E) belongs with which linkage?

ANSWER: PAGE 102

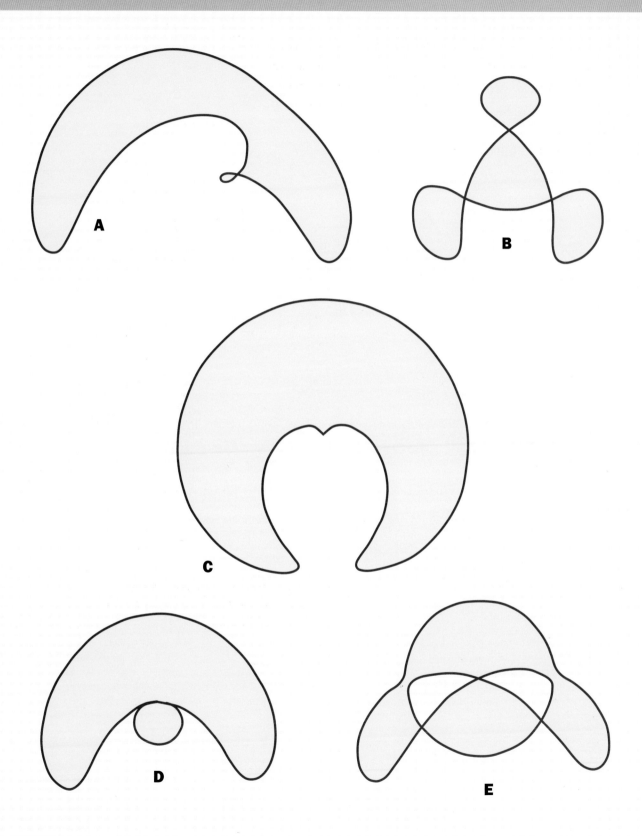

A love affair with patterns is something that starts very early in our lives. Such patterns may take many forms—numerical, geometric, kinetic, behavioral, and so on. As the science of patterns, mathematics affects every aspect of our lives: Abstract patterns are the basis of thinking, of communication, of computations, of society, and even of life itself.

T he scientist in preparing for his work needs three things: mathematics, mathematics, and mathematics.
Wilhelm Conrad Röntgen

❋ Mathematics and geometry today; the science of pattern

For the ancient Greeks, mathematics and geometry were the sciences of numbers and forms. But these definitions of mathematics have been invalid for hundreds of years. In the middle of the 17th century, Isaac Newton in England and Gottfried von Leibniz in Germany independently invented calculus, the study of motion and change, which kickstarted an explosion in mathematical activity.

Contemporary mathematics composes about 80 distinct disciplines, some of which are still being split into further subcategories. So today, rather than focus on numbers, many mathematicians believe that their field is better defined as the science of patterns.

Patterns are everywhere and everyone sees them, but mathematicians see patterns within patterns. Yet, despite the somewhat imposing language used to describe their work, the goal of most mathematicians is to find the simplest explanations for the most complex of patterns.

Part of the magic of mathematics is how a seemingly simple, amusing problem can lead to far-ranging insights. Recognizing the importance of just this kind of thinking has prompted many schools to mix more geometry, topology, and probability into the math curriculum. This is all to the good. Wherever there is relationship and pattern there is mathematics. Did you realize, for instance, that without mathematics there would be no puzzles, no games, no chess?

Popularizing mathematics is not an easy task, however. Giving people hands-on experiences is the only way to make it genuinely accessible to a wider audience. This can be achieved enjoyably through the use of puzzles, problem-solving in general, and hands-on math exhibitions at science museums and science centers all over the world.

What so-called math-afraid people need to understand is that there is fun and beauty in math. And while the subject of math itself may not be difficult, teaching it often is. Teachers need to be able to translate mathematical language into words and pictures that both children and lay people understand.

▼ THE NIGHTMARE BARCODE

This pleasing pattern was created using the same single element—a unit square divided into black-and-white by one of its diagonals and rotated into four different orientations, as shown on the right.

The elements were then randomly distributed in the 32-by-32 square matrix. But something has gone wrong with the pattern. Can you find out what?

ANSWER: PAGE 102

Our brains are marvelously adept at seeing surprising relationships between images, or seeing the same images in different ways. Our perceptions are based on illusions sometimes deceiving us. Yet without our natural talent we would never be able to make sense of our three-dimensional world.

▼ COOL BODIES

Sally had ordered four ice sculptures of the Venus de Milo for her Italian-themed party. Everyone's welcome to attend, but Bring Your Own Vino.

Anyway, she was sure she'd asked for two medium-sized statues, one smaller one, and one larger one. But when the statues had been craned into position against her garden wall, something didn't seem right.

Has Sally received statues in three different sizes or not? Are they in the correct sizes? Which statue is which size?

ANSWER: PAGE **103**

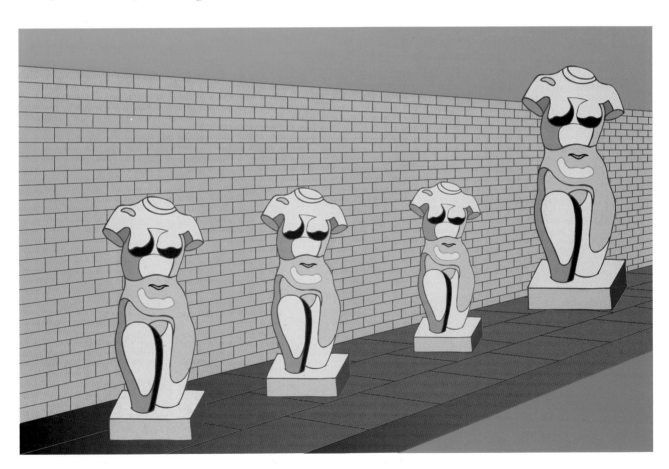

▼ SIZE MATTERS

Logic says the sculpture at the back must be bigger. But is it?

ANSWER: PAGE **103**

Acrossword is just a crossword, right? In fact, they come in several different forms. Next time you see a crossword grid, look at the pattern. Does the grid have half-turn, quarter-turn, left-to-right, or right-to-left symmetry? Or maybe it has no symmetry at all? Here we introduce the symmetrical transformations used in math.

✳ Symmetry

Objects that possess symmetry—the ability to undergo certain geometric transformations without changing form—are found throughout nature. The most perfect natural examples are in the arrangements of atoms and molecules in crystals; a common example is the snowflake, which possesses many axes of symmetry (see page 36). Biological creatures also display a remarkable amount of symmetry. Fivefold or pentagonal symmetry is found, for example, in many marine flowers and animals, such as the sea star, or starfish, which has 5, 10, or even 23 symmetric arms.

We human beings, who are roughly symmetric about one axis, the spine, display bilateral symmetry—the most common form of symmetry in nature.

Objects that look the same as when they are rotated about an axis have rotational symmetry; an equilateral triangle, for instance, will appear identical in three different positions as it rotates around a point at its center. Objects with lateral symmetry, on the other hand, can be reflected on either side of a line or axis without appearing different.

We can easily make symmetrical patterns by folding and cutting paper or by using plane mirrors—what child hasn't made snowflakes or paper dolls in this way? But symmetry is also an enormously important mathematical tool. Scientists could never have determined the structure of viruses and molecules without fully understanding symmetry; neither could they have built the standard model of particle physics.

Symmetry can also be used in three dimensions. For instance, the study of crystallography allows us to examine the arrangement of atoms in a crystal lattice that conform to a repeating pattern. Even if a 2-D photo of a substance is taken, it is possible to work out the 3-D structure. This kind of approach allowed Watson and Crick to discover the structure of DNA.

I see a certain order in the universe and math is one way of making it visible.
May Sarton (1912–1995)

❓ DID YOU KNOW?

Biologists believe that we are programmed to recognize symmetry. They reckon that we judge highly symmetrical faces to be more beautiful than those that are asymmetrical.

✳ Symmetries of the plane—isometries

A transformation of the plane is a motion of its points. Among the possible types of transformations, the most important are the rigid motions, or isometries, which move figures but do not change their shape or size, preserving distances. There are four basic types of isometries of the plane, listed here.

Symmetries are those isometries that transform a figure into itself:

TRANSLATION (sliding without turning)
ROTATION (turn)
REFLECTION (flip or mirror-image)
GLIDE REFLECTION (slide + reflection).

Using these terms, it can thus be said that one congruent figure can be mapped into another by either a translation or rotation, or by a reflection, or a combination of a translation and a reflection.

A combination of a translation and a reflection (or a half-turn and a reflection) is called a glide reflection. An isometry that changes the sense clockwise or counterclockwise is called opposite; one that preserves the sense is direct (reflection or glide reflection).

See the illustrations and explanations below if it's all getting to be too much for you!

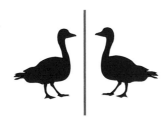

1. TRANSLATION *(parallel displacement).*
The two shapes are identical. They are described as congruent, meaning that by suitable motion one may perfectly be superimposed on the other—in this case by sliding one shape on top of the other.

2. ROTATION *(turn) about a point.*
By turning the shape around a point the two shapes are superimposed.

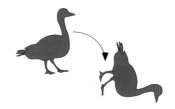

3. REFLECTION *(flip).*
Rotation about a straight line. For instance, what about these two shapes? One is a mirror-image of the other. No motion keeping the shapes in the plane will superimpose them. One must be lifted out of the plane into the third dimension, turned over, and replaced in the plane.

4. GLIDE REFLECTION.
A combination of a translation and a reflection.

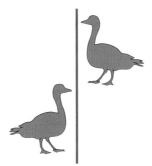

That there exists a basic unity within the diversity of processes in nature is one of the oldest observations of humankind. The ancients attributed this unity to a single Creator. In recent times, this concept has become basic to both art and science. G.D. Birkhoff, an American mathematician, in 1928 developed a theory of esthetic measure based on this principle, which he called "order in complexity." The measure of his esthetic value is in direct proportion to order and in inverse proportion to complexity.

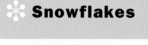

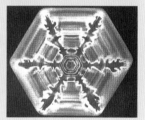

✳ Snowflakes

The most fundamental concept in nature is symmetry. Symmetry characterizes pattern.

Snowflakes are the most beautiful and mysterious examples of symmetry in nature. There are billions of snowflakes, all of which are different, but all of which repeat their sixfold pattern. A snowflake has six reflectional symmetries, and also six rotational symmetries: through 0, 60, 120, 180, 240, and 300 degrees. (Rotational symmetry through 0 degrees is important to mathematicians. Leaving out this "trivial symmetry" is like trying to do arithmetic without zero.)

All snowflakes are united by their basic hexagonal pattern, and each snowflake is restricted to one pattern, repeated and reflected twelve times.

" *U* *nder the microscope, I found that snowflakes were miracles of beauty; and it seemed a shame that this beauty should not be seen and appreciated by others. Every crystal was a masterpiece of design and no one design was ever repeated. When a snowflake melted, that design was forever lost. Just that much beauty was gone, without leaving any record behind...*
Wilson "Snowflake" Bentley (1865–1931)
Bentley was the first person to photograph a single snow crystal in 1885. He went on to photograph more than 5,000 snowflakes during his lifetime, not finding any two alike. **"**

▼ DUDENEY'S QUILT

A beautiful quilt was sewn together originally with unit square pieces. Unfortunately, the eight middle square pieces were damaged and had to be removed, forming a long, rectangular hole.

Can the quilt be repaired by cutting it along the square grid into two parts that can be sewn together to form a new quilt without holes?

ANSWER: PAGE 103

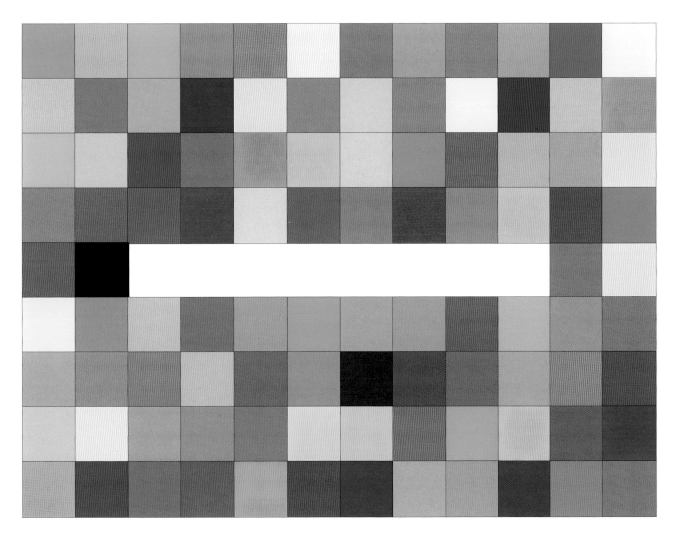

In mathematics, frieze patterns have what is called "translational symmetry." If a design is formed by translation (see page 35) in only one direction it is called a frieze. The repeating patterns may have rotational, reflectional, or glide reflectional symmetry. Given the isometries of the plane, there are seven unique classifications of frieze patterns.

▲ TRICKY TAPESTRY

In this frieze pattern, numerical values are translated into colors as shown. Observing the pattern, can you discover the rules of how they were created, and add the missing colors in the blank spaces? Hint: Look at groups of four diamonds.

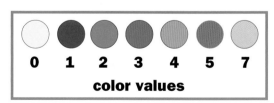

color values

PROF. H.S.M. COXETER (1907–2003)

Harold Scott MacDonald (Donald) Coxeter was born in London and educated at the University of Cambridge. In 1936, he took an appointment at the University of Toronto, where he was celebrated for over 60 years of work. He is considered one of the greatest geometers of the last century. His contributions to geometry, combinatorics, recreational mathematics, and mathematical games are enormous, and he is highly regarded in the field of frieze patterns, which he wrote about in his celebrated book Convex Polytopes.

I **am extremely fortunate for being paid for what I would have done anyway.**
Prof. H.S.M. Coxeter

▼ RUG-GED ARITHMETIC

Once again, numerical values are translated into colors as shown. Observing the pattern, can you discover the rules of how they were created, and add the missing colors in the blank spaces?

ANSWER: PAGE **105**

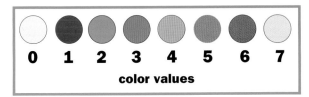

0   1   2   3   4   5   6   7
color values

Mazes have been around as long as man himself. Some basic maze designs have been found in Sardinia dating from nearly 4,000 years ago. A famous example of an ancient maze was that of the minotaur in the palace of Knossos.

▲ ON THE GARDEN PATH?

The garden above is divided by a non-intersecting curved fence into two regions—an inside and an outside. Only three parts of the garden are visible, however; the remainder is covered by trees.

The three cats preying on the mice are all outside the fence. The fence cannot be crossed.

How many mice can be caught by the cats? Hint: How many fences separate the inside from the outside?

ANSWER: PAGE *106*

▲ INTERGALACTIC COMBAT

Five fleets of starships are ready for combat: the yellow, red, green, blue, and pink fleets, each consisting of eight ships.

Your object is to distribute the 40 ships on the console screen at right, one ship in each square, so that when the laser beams from all ships are fired horizontally, vertically, and diagonally, they hit only the enemy ships, and no beam can hit a ship of one's own color. Note that the beams pass through ships—that is, they do not stop at the first ship but hit all the ships in the beam's straight path.

ANSWER: PAGE **107**

Laboratory mice are well known for their maze-solving skills, and rabbits dig complex warrens to deter predators and provide a base for their community. Here we invite you to discover the lesser-known abilities of ants and ladybugs to traverse mazes…

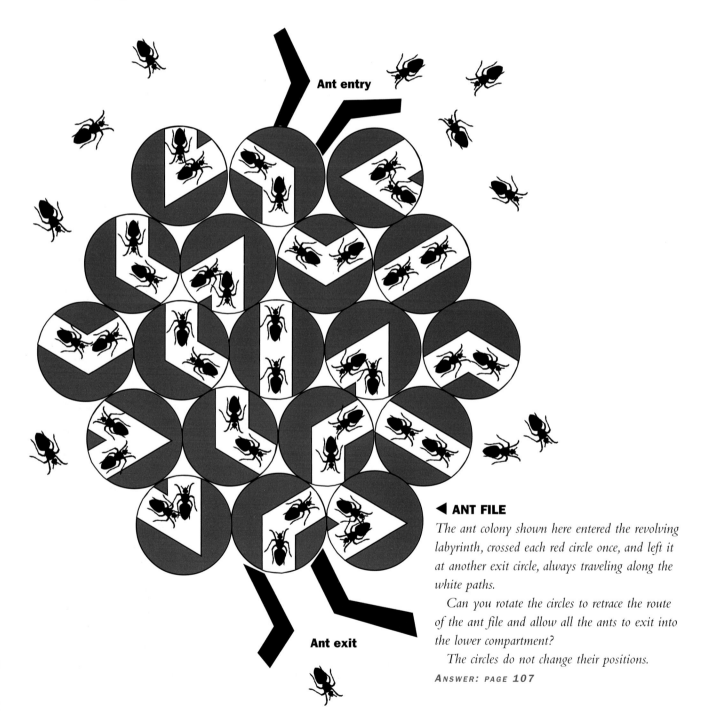

Ant entry

Ant exit

◄ ANT FILE

The ant colony shown here entered the revolving labyrinth, crossed each red circle once, and left it at another exit circle, always traveling along the white paths.

Can you rotate the circles to retrace the route of the ant file and allow all the ants to exit into the lower compartment?

The circles do not change their positions.

ANSWER: PAGE **107**

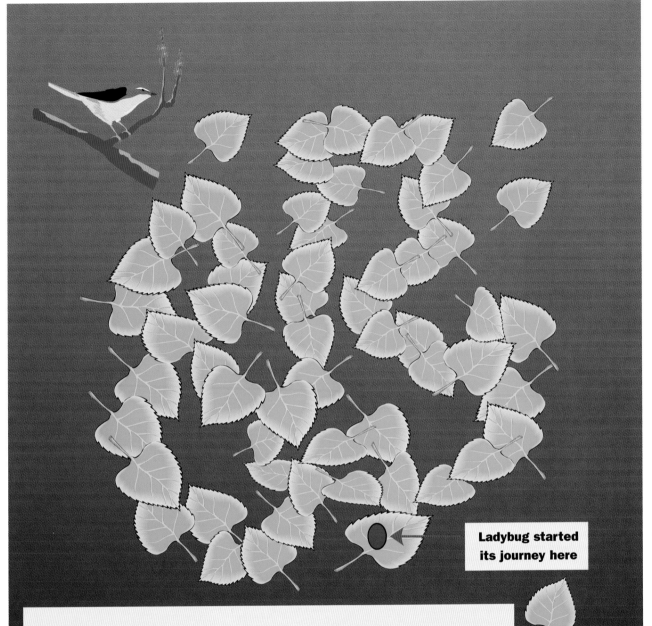

Ladybug started its journey here

▲ LADYBUG IN HIDING

The bird at top left is looking for a nice juicy ladybug that she saw crawling around on these leaves. The ladybug started on the leaf shown at bottom then traveled once across every available overlap between one leaf and an adjacent leaf. She stopped when there were no new "overlaps" to visit. As a result she visited every leaf in the maze once, except for the junctions, which she visited twice. Under which leaf is the ladybug hiding?

ANSWER: PAGE 108

I t's possible that in the future we could travel to places far, far away thanks to wormholes. If we imagine our world as a sheet of paper folded into a C-shape, a wormhole would provide a shortcut between the two ends of the paper. Not only could wormholes allow us to travel many light-years from Earth in a fraction of the time, we could even travel through time!

▼ I-SPY

The vigilant interplanetary security officer below followed an intruder on his computer screen. The alien spyship entered his planetary system from the top, and in one continuous path crossed all the established routes between the planets indicated by yellow circles. He visited all the planets, collecting secret information on the way, never crossing a route more than once, and with the obvious intention of leaving the system as quickly as possible and unobserved. But defense forces are waiting at the point of his intended departure and the chances of escape are scarce.

Can you guess at which exit point the interplanetary defense forces are waiting?

ANSWER: PAGE **109**

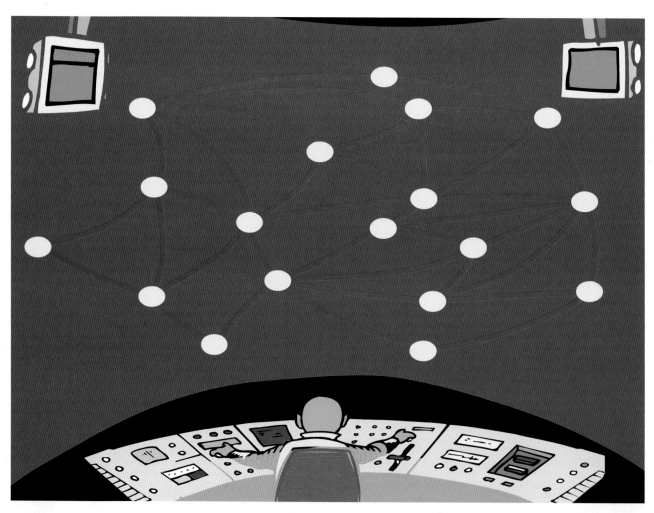

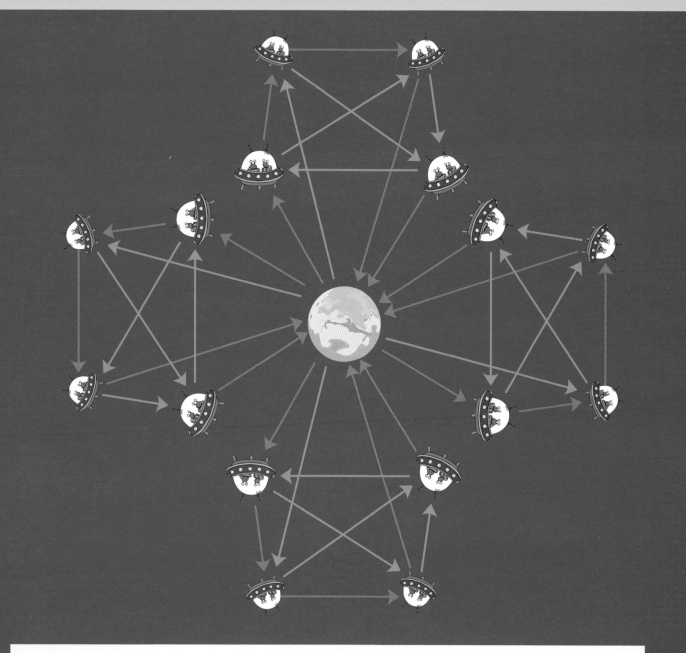

▲ FLEET ADMIRAL

The fleet of 16 alien space ships shown above is lost in space, each ship trying to find its route to the home planet shown in the middle. From ground control they have received the above route map, marked with red and blue arrows.

It conceals a secret color sequence code consisting of a combination of red and blues:

??????

Following this unique code according to the colors and directions of the arrows, all the ships will be guided by their automatic computers back to their landing bases, no matter where they are.

Red–blue–red, for example, is wrong as it would lead only half the ships home. Can you discover the correct secret color code and guide all the ships home?

ANSWER: PAGE **110**

Three dimensions seem normal and manageable, yet some scientists believe that space is made up of ten dimensions (plus the 11th dimension of time)! In these puzzles, you'll be relieved that we've found ways of representing three dimensions as two-dimensional drawings.

▼ LOST IN SPACE

This huge space station is constructed from 39 giant spherical modules, interconnected by a network of transparent cylindrical passages as shown below.

In their spare time, the intergalactic crew and visitors try to traverse the whole space station, visiting each module and never retracing their journey through the interconnecting passages.

Is this possible, and, if so, how can it be done?

Your task is to re-create their journey, starting at one of the modules and, without lifting your pencil from the page, visiting each module at least once but without going over any interconnecting channel more than once. Some of the interconnecting passages may be left untraversed.

ANSWER: PAGE 111

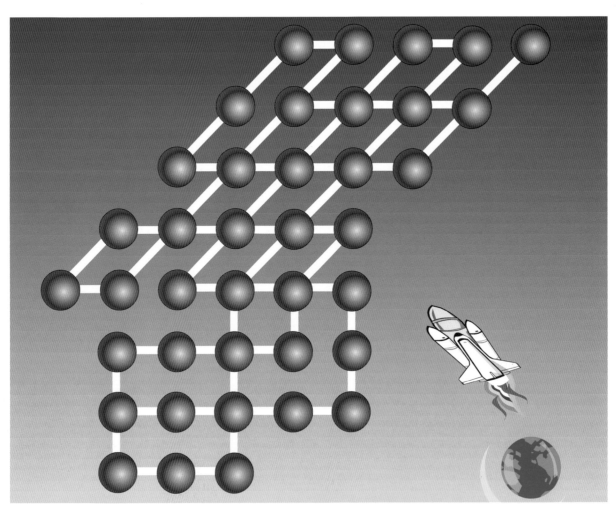

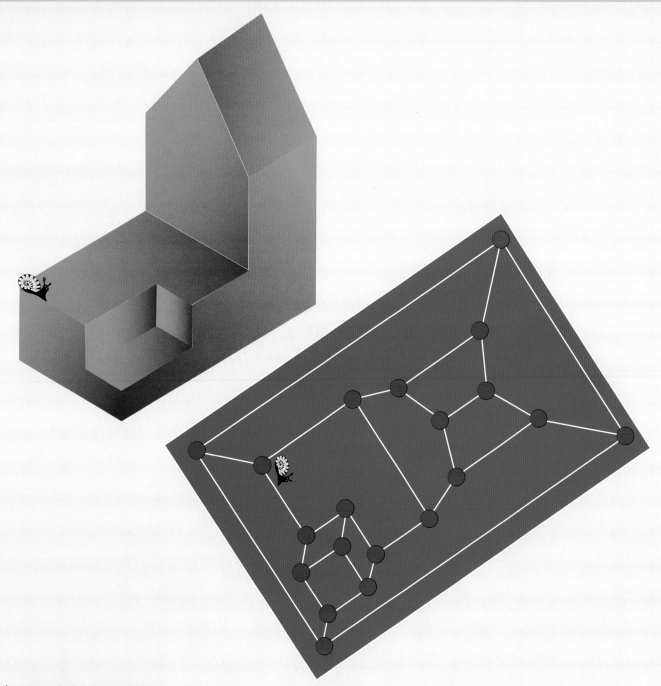

▲ SCHLEGEL'S SHORTCUT

Starting at the corner shown, can you find a route for the snail along the edges of this three-dimensional solid object that will visit each corner only once, with no edge retraced? Such a route is called a Hamiltonian circuit.

It can be cumbersome to solve such problems looking at the

three-dimensional representation of objects, because some edges and corners are hidden. So to help you we have created a topologically equivalent two-dimensional representation of the object, called a Schlegel diagram, on which the solution can be more easily worked out.

ANSWER: PAGE 112

If you have arguments about map-reading, fear not, because you're probably doing just as well as a computer. Route-planning is one of the most complex calculations a computer can do—it's easy enough for a handful of cities, but when more locations are added the calculations multiply at an astonishing rate. See how you get on with these tricky travel teasers.

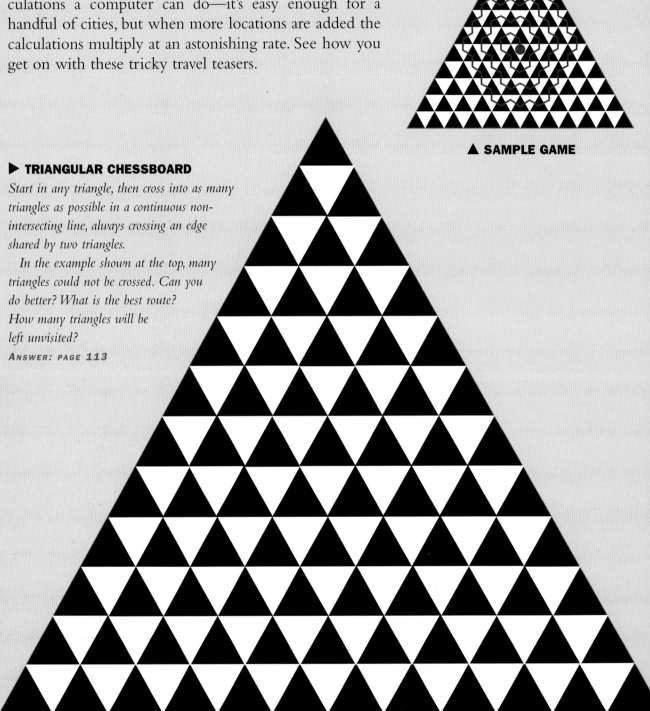

▲ **SAMPLE GAME**

▶ **TRIANGULAR CHESSBOARD**

Start in any triangle, then cross into as many triangles as possible in a continuous non-intersecting line, always crossing an edge shared by two triangles.

In the example shown at the top, many triangles could not be crossed. Can you do better? What is the best route? How many triangles will be left unvisited?

ANSWER: PAGE **113**

▼ LINEUP

How many lines will you be able to trace from left to right, just by looking, before you lose track? Stability of attention is required. This is the ability to direct your attention for a long period toward something, combined with resistance to fatigue and distraction.

ANSWER: PAGE 114

Any number of players can play this ingenious color-shape game. The aim is to collect three cards. If you don't wish to cut up the pages of the book, a color photocopy will work just as well.

▼ GEOMETRY LOTTERY

Cut out the 32 triangular cards shown (or make a color copy to cut). Each set of 16 contains four shapes in a different combination of four colors. Also cut out spinner parts A and B. Push a pin through the middle of both pieces—we suggest you use something soft (for example, a cork) on the underside to avoid injury from the sharp point. If you flick part B, it should now spin freely over the top of the color wheel. If it doesn't, widen its pinhole a little.

How to play:

Play the game with any number of players. First make sure the 32 cards are well mixed and placed face up on the table in easy reach of all the players. Players alternate turns to spin the code-selector spinner. Once it stops, the object of each player is to be the first to grab the card or cards identified by the code on the spinner, that is, the card on which the four shapes appear in the colors indicated by the spinner. (The sample spinner opposite indicates the card showing a red triangle, a green square, a yellow hexagon, and a blue circle, which is the first card shown at top left on this page.) The first player to collect three cards is the winner.

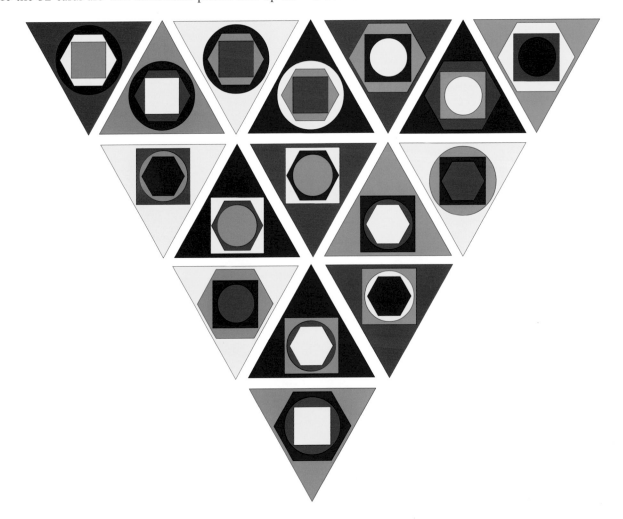

CODE-SELECTOR SPINNER

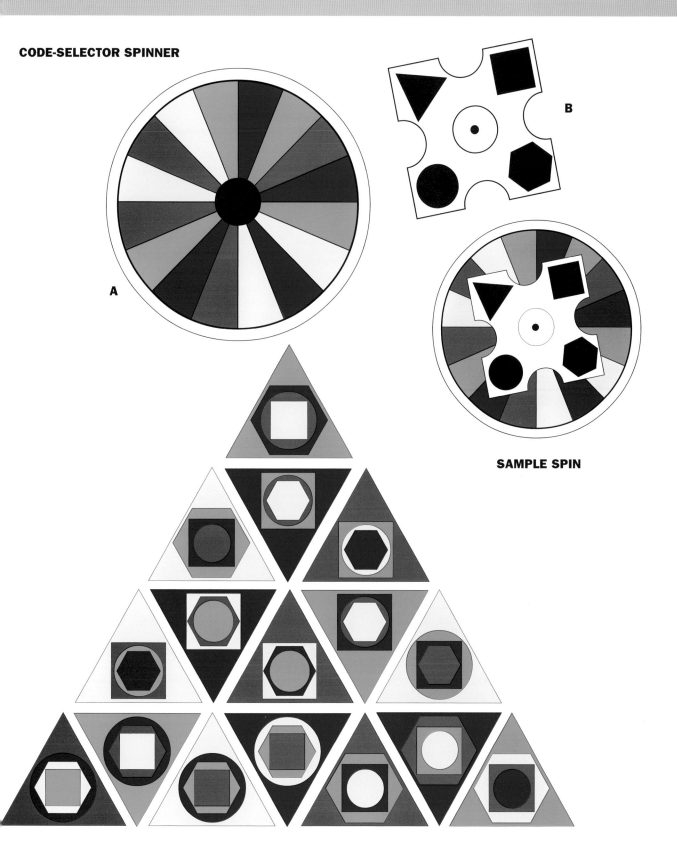

A

B

SAMPLE SPIN

Point-to-point races are cross-country steeplechases where amateur horse riders race over a marked course with various jumps and obstacles. As it happens, these point-to-point puzzles have certain obstacles to overcome too.

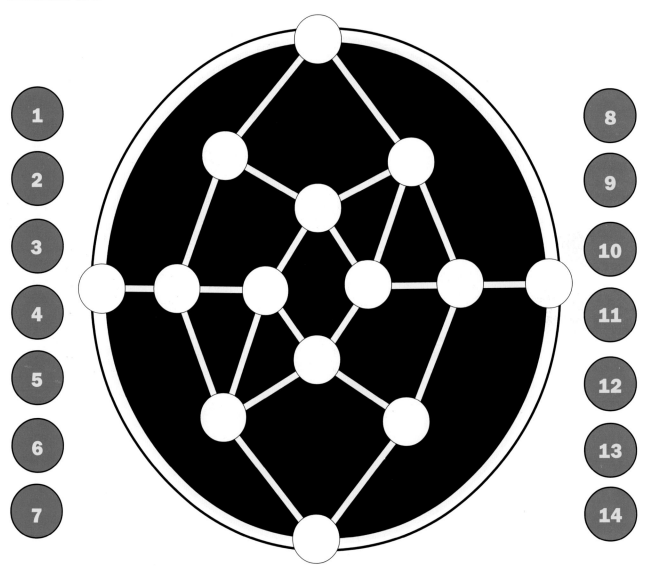

▲ GLOBE-TROTTING

Can you visit the 14 circles within the map in succession along a continuous line, visiting each circle just once and returning to the point from which you started?

ANSWER: PAGE **114**

▶ **RIGHT TO THE EDGE**

How many colors will you need to color each straight line between two gray endpoints, so that no two lines of the same color will meet at any endpoint?

ANSWER: PAGE 115

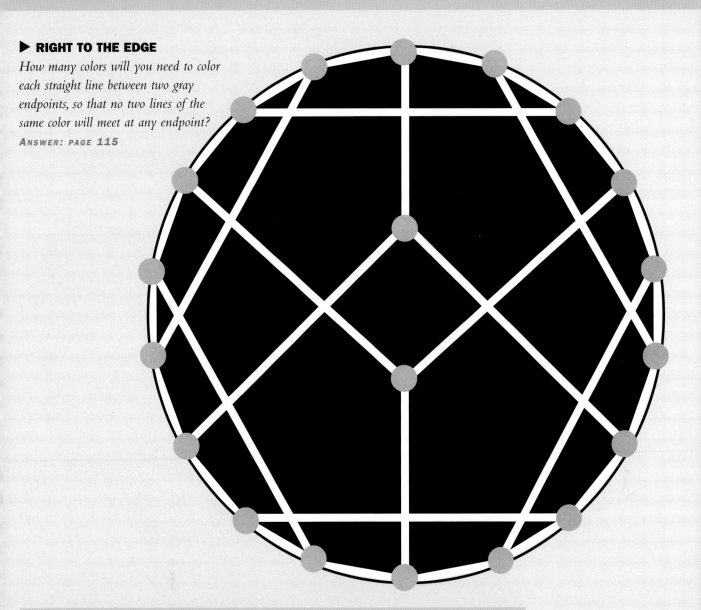

✳ Edge-coloring of graphs

The problem of edge-coloring of graphs arises in a great variety of scheduling applications. It is typically associated with reducing the number of rounds needed to complete a given set of tasks, so it is a useful skill for everyone to master.

For example, consider a situation in which we need to schedule a given set of two-person interviews. We can construct a graph whose ver- tices are the people, with the edges representing the pairs of people who want to meet. An edge- coloring of the graph defines the schedule. The colors represent the different time periods, with all meetings of the same color happening simultaneously.

The minimum number of colors needed to edge-color a graph is called its "edge-chromatic number" or "chromatic index."

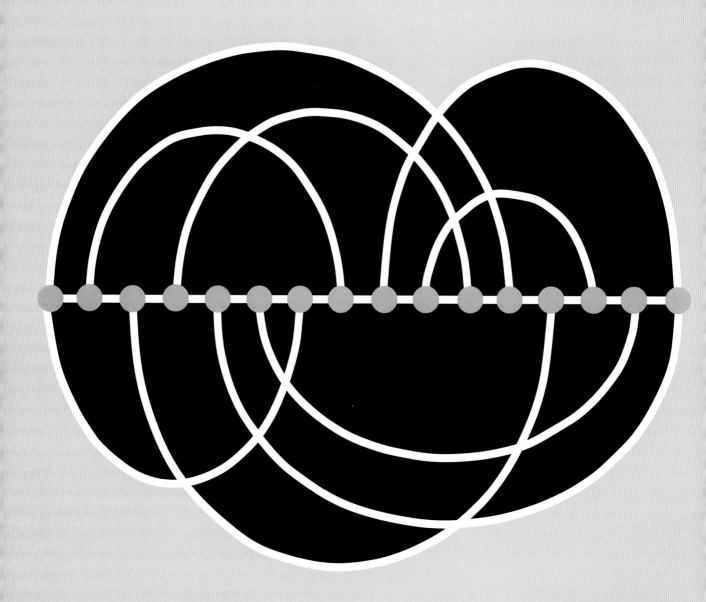

▲ HOOP HOOP HOORAY!

*How many colors will you need to color each line between two
gray endpoints, so that no two lines of the same color will meet at
any endpoint?*

ANSWER: PAGE 116

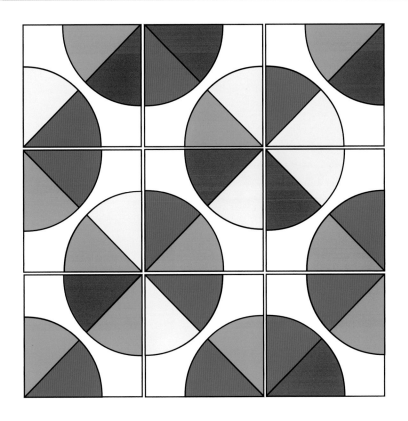

◀ ROUNDABOUTS

Copy and cut out the nine colored squares at the top, each of which contains parts of a colored circle. (Or color in the blank grid below if you don't want to cut up the book.)

The object of the game is to rearrange the pieces to form two complete circles, each composed of four different colors and with colors matching all along the touching edges. Pieces can be rotated.

For a bonus credit, make sure every side of the 3x3 square contains at least three colors.

ANSWER: PAGE **117**

▲ PIPELINE PUZZLE

Can you color all the lines between two points using four colors, so that at every point there will be four different-colored lines meeting? To play as a game, players alternate coloring lines. The first player unable to color a line loses the game.

ANSWER: PAGE 118

Studying problems such as the one below has helped devise networks such as the Internet. Even a single email may travel in different parts via different routes and be reassembled before hitting your inbox.

▶ NETWORKING

Color each vertex (white circle) of the graph so that no edge (black line) will connect two identically colored vertices. What is the smallest number of colors needed to achieve this objective?

ANSWER: PAGE **119**

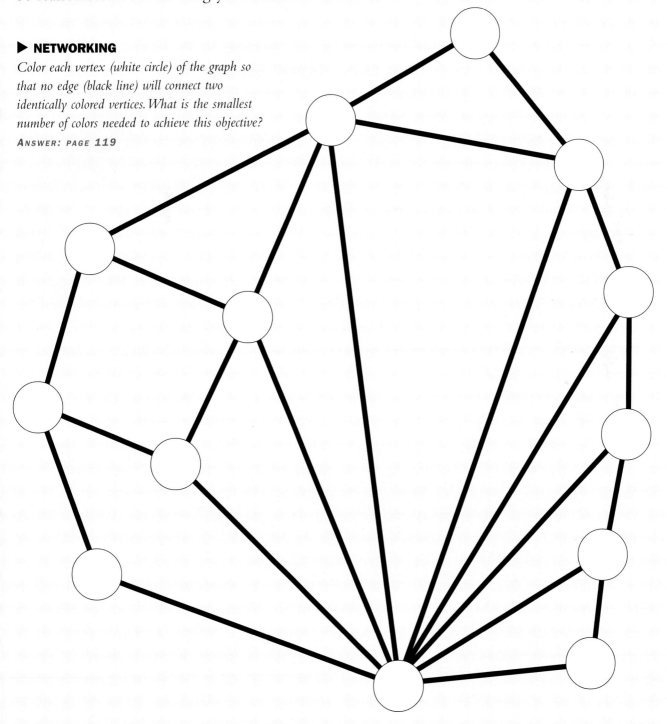

It comes as no surprise that soccer, the world's most popular sport, has provided the inspiration for dozens of table and pencil-and-paper games. Here is one for you to play that is very simple but challenging.

STARTING POSITIONS

▲ SOCCER

For this game you need 11 players for each team plus a ball. The players can be represented by disks in two colors or two sets of different coins, etc. The ball can be a small white button. Initially, the two sets of playing pieces are set up as shown above. The rules are very simple:

1. Players can move any distance along straight lines in any direction. They cannot jump over another player or the ball.

2. To make a kick, a player travels along a line until he meets the ball. He then stays on the spot just before the ball and the ball is kicked forward in the same direction, any

desired distance. After kicking the ball the player stays on the spot before the ball.

3. Normally the ball may not pass over the heads of any of the other players. However, if a player is starting his move from a point next to the ball, he is allowed to kick it over the heads of his opponents. In this case the ball can travel up to a maximum of two dots beyond the last man on the line of play.

4. When a goal is scored, the loser has the next kick off (the game is first reset).

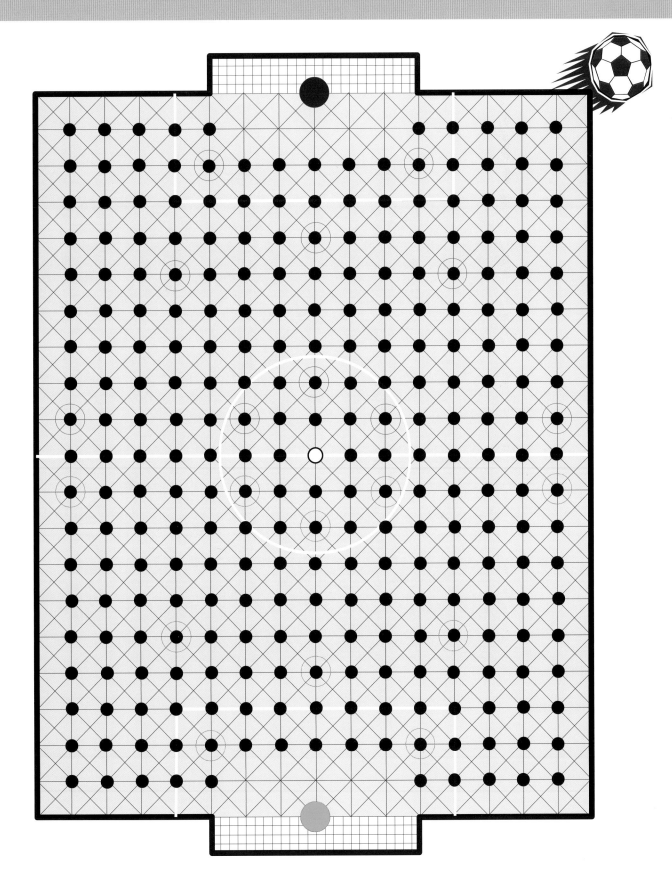

The phrase to "turn turtle" usually means to overturn a boat. But in this game, the turtles take turns to race from the top to the bottom of the path. Place your bets on who'll win— red or green?

START

START

Permitted lines

▶ **SAMPLE GAME**

FINISH

FINISH

▲ TURTLE TURNS

This is a paper-and-pencil game. Players choose a side and color. The two turtles start at the top, as shown, and alternate moves. A move is made by coloring one of the white lines along adjacent square tiles in that player's colors. The object is to complete an unbroken line without loops to the finish. Lines may also be added to the opponent's line to interfere or slow down his or her advance. You may not add a line to your opponent's route if that line makes it impossible for him or her to reach the finish. Intersection of the two paths is not allowed, nor is it permitted to cross any line more than once.

The sample game above shows green winning.

▼ THE GAMEBOARD

Start

Start

Finish

Finish

Color away with these problems from John Horton Conway. The resulting combinations from coloring the sections of a pentagon are called quintominoes—see how many you can find at the first attempt.

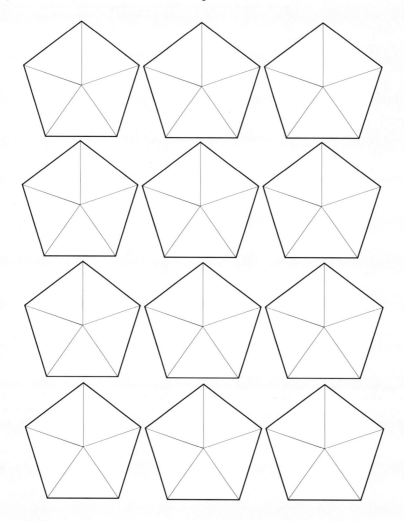

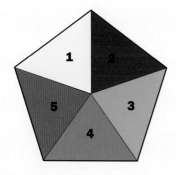

▲ QUINTOMINO QUERY

There are twelve different ways to color the sections of a regular pentagon using one color for each section. Can you color the whole set above?

One example has been provided. Rotations and reflections are not counted as different combinations.

ANSWER: PAGE 120

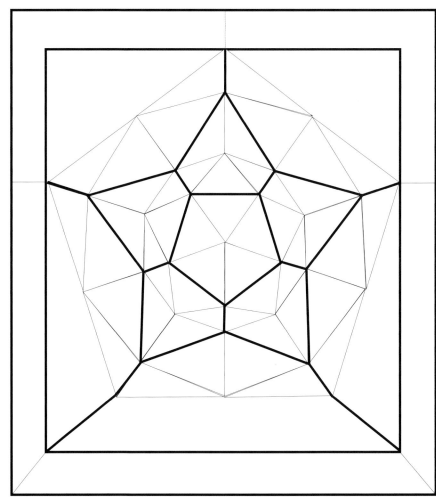

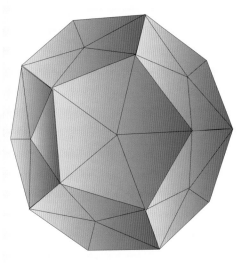

**Regular
Dodecahedron**

▲ QUINTOMINO DODECAHEDRON

*A regular dodecahedron is a three-dimensional solid with
12 regular pentagons as its faces.*

*Conway asked if it was possible to color the edges of a
dodecahedron so that each of the 12 quintominoes would
appear on one of its faces. Can you find a way to place the
12 quintominoes on the sides of a dodecahedron by coloring
the diagram above? Faces meeting at edges are the same color.*

*You can try to solve the puzzle by constructing a 3-D
solid or by a Schlegel diagram of dodecahedron in the plane,
which is topologically identical to the 3-dimensional solid.*

*In the distorted diagram note that the back face is stretched
to become the outer edge of the diagram. Hint: you will find
that faces meeting at edges will share the same color.*

Answer: page 120

Who'd have thought that matchsticks could be so versatile? As well as the more familiar puzzles involving Roman numerals or that ask you to form a given number of squares and triangles, here we're investigating essentially similar ways in which matches can be joined together.

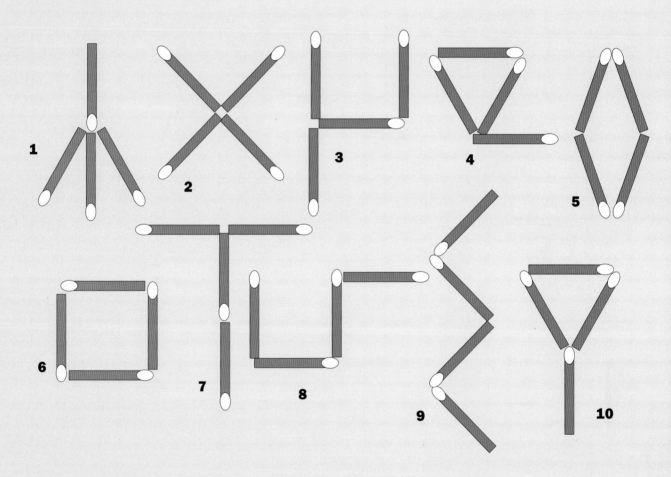

▲ MIX AND MATCH

Four matches provide five possible topologically different configurations, taking the following conditions into account:
1. Matchsticks may touch only at their ends;
2. Matchsticks are flat on the plane.

Note: Once a configuration is formed, it can be transformed in an infinite number of ways into topologically equivalent
structures, by deforming it without separating its connections at the joints. Each configuration is shown here in two topologically equivalent configurations.

Can you match the five pairs?

ANSWER: PAGE 120

▼ MORE MUDDLED MATCHES

This time we have five matches, giving 12 possible topologically different configurations, as shown. Can you find the 12 pairs, again taking into account the conditions noted on page 64?

ANSWER: PAGE *120*

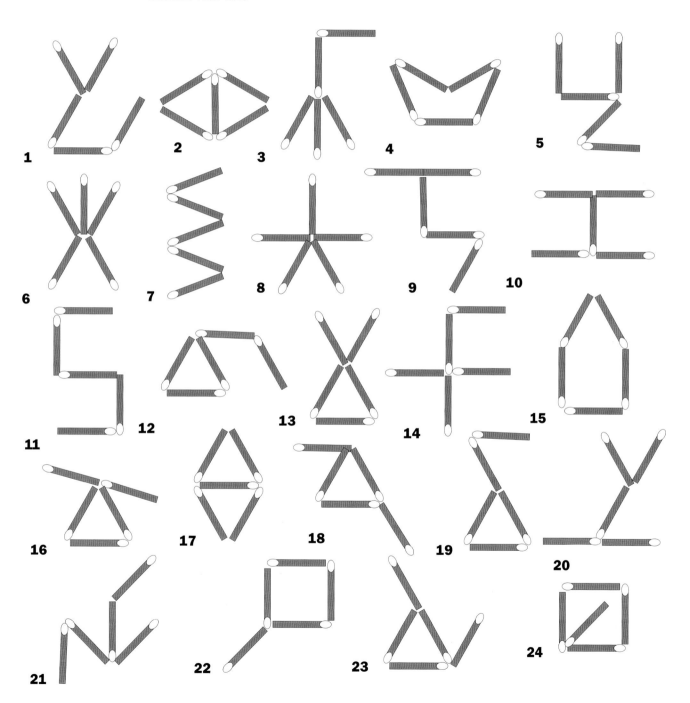

1

2

3

4

5

6

7

8

9

10

11

12

13

14

15

16

17

18

19

20

21

22

23

24

So the natural progression now is to investigate net-works of six matches. As well as providing a puzzle, you can also use this investigation as a tactical game for two or more players.

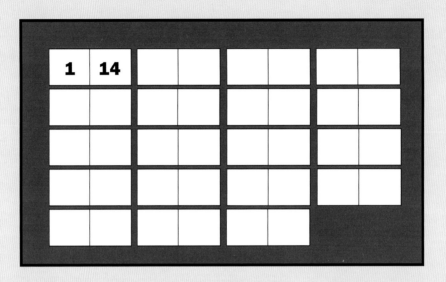

▶ MITCH-MATCH

The puzzle With six matches there are essentially 19 topologically different configurations (graphs), taking these conditions into account:

1. The matchsticks may touch only at their ends.

2. Matchsticks are flat on the plane.

Note: Once you have formed a configuration, you can have fun transforming it in an infinite number of ways into topologically equivalent figures, by deforming it without separating its connections at the joints.

Each configuration is shown in two topologically equivalent forms. Can you find the 19 pairs? For example, card number 1 matches card number 14.

ANSWER: PAGE **121**

The game This is a game you can easily set up, providing lots of fun plus the opportunity to learn a little about graph theory. It consists of a set of 38 cards, which you have to copy and cut out. As well as the set of cards you will need six matchsticks or similar items.

How to play:

Initially the six matchsticks form a straight line. Shuffle the cards in a pack and place them face down on the table. The first player takes the top three cards. He or she then has three moves with which to change the positions of the matchsticks to re-create the revealed cards. The re-created cards are kept by the player as his or her score.

A move is constituted by picking up a stick and placing it in a new position. However, a player may also make as many rotations as required, in the following way: pivoting a stick about one of its ends, provided this end is attached to the remainder of the graph. A stick that is attached at both ends may not be rotated.

Thus, a card can be kept as a point if the corresponding graphs are recreated by one, two, or three moves, and any number of rotations.

The next player now takes the next three cards and so on until all the cards are taken. The winner is the player who has the most cards.

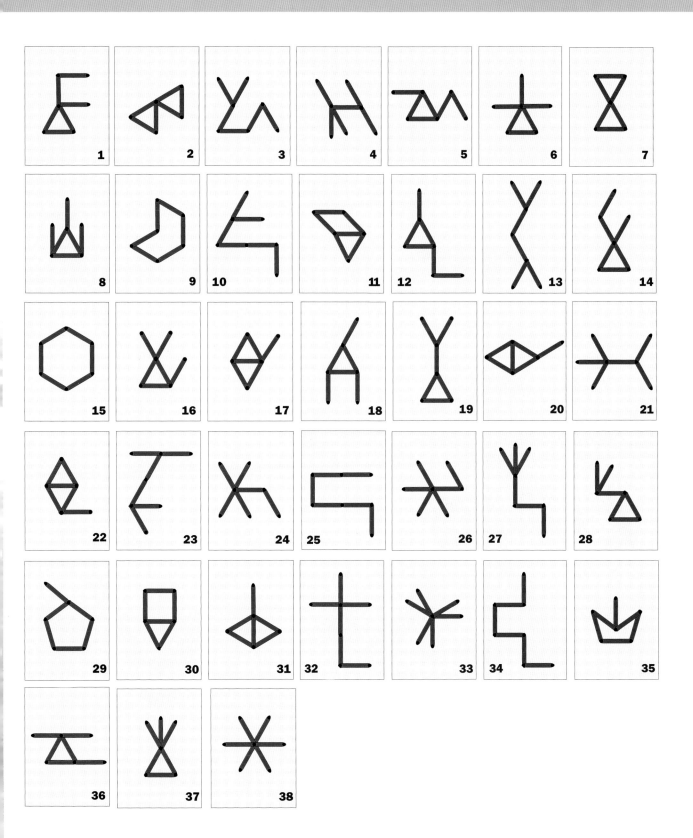

It is well known that human beings can be left- or right-handed, but did you know that many important molecules exist in two forms that are mirror images of each other? This property is called chirality, taken from the Greek word for "hand." In this two-sided game, you'll need to have a good sense of direction if you're to survive.

◄ **ARROW ARMIES**

The initial configuration of the playing pieces for the two players is shown on the right.

The object of the game is to remove all the opposing player's pieces by landing on the positions they occupy.

Players alternate moves; each player has a choice of making either one or two moves during his or her turn, using only one playing piece. The turns can be:

1. *directional—moving the piece forward one, two, or three places following the direction of the arrow and the value of the piece (values are indicated by the dots, so, for example, three dots indicate three places);*

2. *rotational—rotating the piece left or right, one, two, or three quarter-turns according to the piece value, so that the arrow will be pointing in a new direction, or;*

3. *combinational—two moves, using both a forward move (always in the direction of the arrow), plus a rotational move within one turn, in any order.*

NOTE: *A player may not move to or jump across a position occupied by his or her own playing pieces, but it is permitted to jump over an opponent's pieces.*

A player may take two of the opposite player's pieces in one turn if they are in a direct line from the attacking player's piece.

If both players are left with only one playing piece toward the end of the game, then a rule will apply whereby neither player can use the same move more than once at any one position.

▼ **GAMEBOARD**

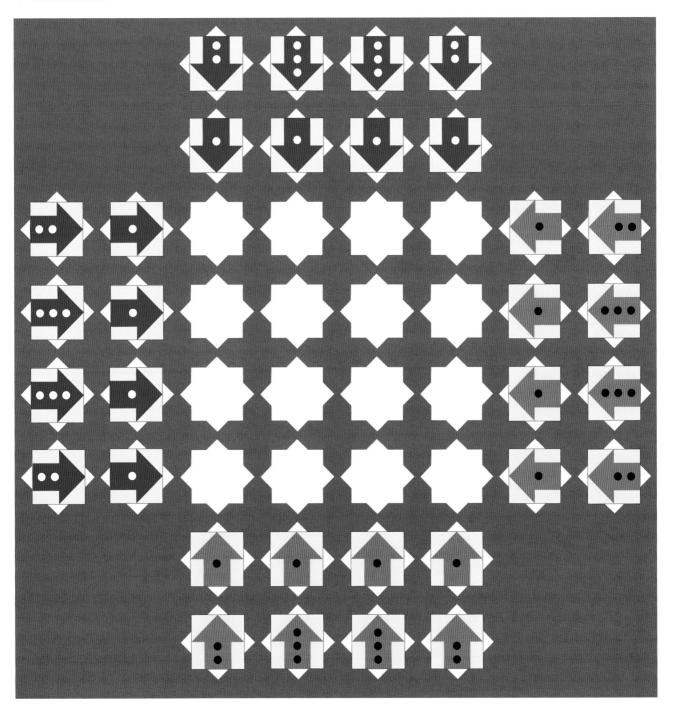

In days of old, it was quite common for one's arrow-firing equipment to snap and so require a repair, hence the popular saying "another string to your bow" for a backup plan. In this game, the arrows are of a much less lethal nature.

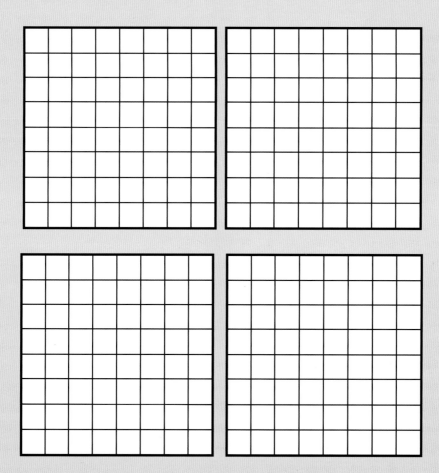

▲ AIM YOUR ARROWS

The puzzle Choose and color one arrow in each box of the grid, as shown in the first box on page 73, so that no two arrows point in the same direction in any row or any column, all the way along until the grid is filled (you can use the blank grids above to create your own games). **Answer: page 121**

The game In a competition game, any number of players alternate turns coloring one arrow in a box in a strong color, say, red. The rest of the arrows in the box are then eliminated in black, as shown in the first box of the gameboard.

Again, no two arrows should be pointing in the same direction not only in any row or column, but also in all diagonals (including all the smaller diagonals in all directions, not just the two main diagonals). The first player unable to color an arrow on his or her turn loses the game.

▼ **THE GAMEBOARD**

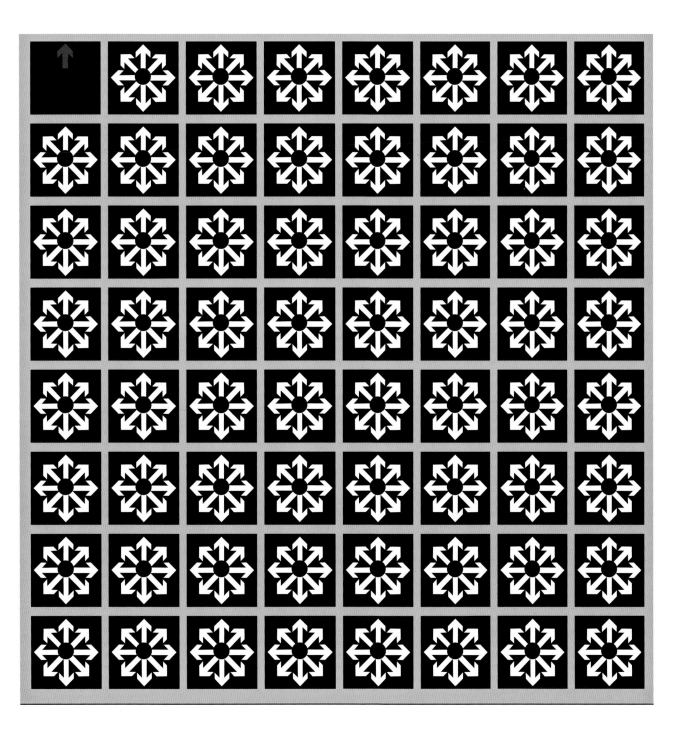

Balance can be achieved by the proportion, or comparative relationship, of one area to another. Asymmetrical forms that seem beautiful to us have balance, or dynamic symmetry. Here we investigate this fundamental concept further.

THE GOLDEN RATIO

The golden ratio, golden section, or the divine proportion, is denoted by the Greek letter phi (ϕ):

$$\phi = \frac{-1+\sqrt{5}}{2} \approx 0.618$$

You may have previously encountered the Fibonacci number sequence. The golden ratio and Fibonacci numbers are closely related. Do you know how?

(ANSWER: PAGE **122**)

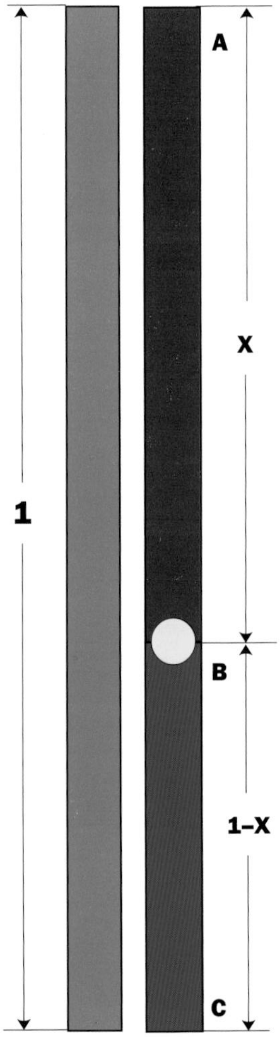

✳ Magical numbers

Take a look at the diagram on the left. We've drawn two lines of 1 unit in length. Let's "snap" the second line into two pieces. If one piece is X, it follows that the remaining part must be 1 – X. We want to know for what size of X the following condition holds:

Ratio of 1 to X is the same as ratio of X to 1 – X

Mathematically, we can write this as:

$$\frac{1}{X} = \frac{X}{1-X}$$
$$X^2 = 1 - X$$

The equation has two solutions

$$X1 = \frac{-1+\sqrt{5}}{2} \approx 0.618$$

$$X2 = \frac{-1-\sqrt{5}}{2} \approx -1.618$$

but the length must be positive, so the first is valid.

Hence, X = 0.618 (approximately). Therefore, the ratio of 1 to 0.618 is the same as the ratio of 0.618 to (1 – 0.618) = 0.382. This proportion is the golden ratio.

A

X

1

B

1–X

C

Geometry has two great treasures: One is the theorem of Pythagoras; the other the division of a line into extreme and mean ratio. The first we may compare to a measure of gold; the second we name a precious jewel.
Euclid

✳ Dynamic symmetry

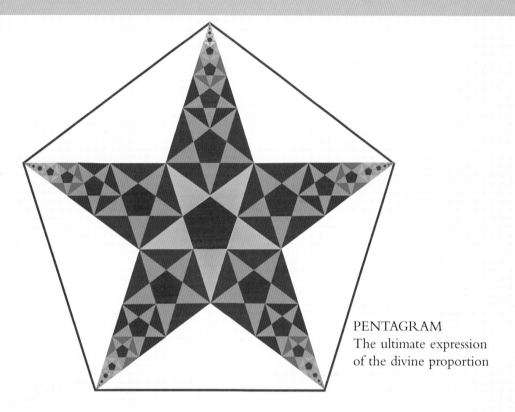

PENTAGRAM
The ultimate expression
of the divine proportion

Where would you place a point on a line to divide the line in the most pleasing and meaningful way?

Among the multitude of possible points on the line, there is one very special point that divides the line into a mathematical ratio called the golden section, or golden ratio, which since antiquity has played an important role not only in mathematics, but also in esthetics, architecture, and art.

Dynamic symmetry is an application of geometry with the golden ratio in the main role. It is a pleasing type of symmetry dominating nature and man. Eudoxus, a Greek mathematician, was the first to try to find out why the golden section was so pleasing. He is said to have gone around with a stick, asking his friends to mark it at the point they found the most pleasing. He was astonished to find that the majority of people agreed almost exactly on the point that divided the stick into two parts in the golden ratio. He also worked out the mathematics of the golden ratio, expressing it by a formula, and calling it phi, after Phidias, an artist who used it extensively in his sculptures.

The divine section or golden ratio was defined by the ancient Greeks, in terms of geometry, as the point that divided a straight line into two parts, such that the ratio of the smaller part to the larger is exactly equal to the ratio of the larger to the whole line.

The value of the golden ratio, or phi, is approximately 0.618—an irrational number. Phi is the only positive number that becomes its own reciprocal by adding one, as follows:
$$^1/_{phi} = 1.618.$$

The Greeks believed that art and architecture based on this ratio is unusually pleasing to the eye. They must have been surprised and greatly enforced in this belief when they found this ratio in the pentagram, the sacred sign of the Pythagoreans, and in connection with the Fibonacci number sequence.

An enormous amount of literature has been accumulated around the golden ratio over the years, with arguments that it is the key to the understanding of all morphology (including human anatomy), art, architecture, and even music, etc.

Who would have believed that this innocent-looking line division, which Euclid defined for purely geometrical purposes, would have such enormous consequences in fields as diverse as science, mathematics, and art?

Were you aware that the golden ratio, or phi (φ), plays an important role as a fundamental building block in nature? Plants, animals, and even human beings possess dimensional properties according to phi.

DIVINE PROPORTIONS IN NATURE

Why does nature like using phi (φ) in so many ways? Can you discover where the golden ratio is hiding in the following examples?

HONEYBEES

Can you guess the proportion of females to males in a honeybee community?

ANSWER: PAGE **122**

NAUTILUS SHELL

The Nautilus is a member of an ancient group of mollusks that lives in the sea, related to squids and octopuses. As it grows it makes each new chamber larger than the last, sealing each old chamber when abandoned for a new one. How might this be related to φ?

ANSWER: PAGE **122**

SUNFLOWER

Can you believe that φ even affects sunflowers? To find out how, go to the answer page.

ANSWER: PAGE **122**

Model proportions

Try to measure the distance from the tip of your head to the floor. Then divide that by the distance from your belly-button to the floor. Will the result be the same as that of the model?

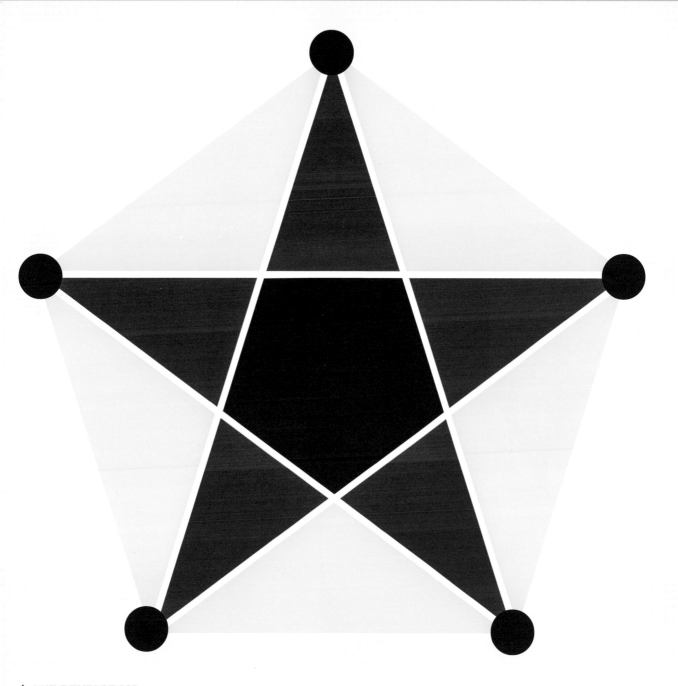

▲ THE PENTAGRAM

The pentagram, or the pentacle, as the ancients called it, a five-pointed pentagonal star, was the secret symbol of Pythagoras and his followers. It hides the secret through which the golden rectangle (see page 78) and the golden triangle can be created. It was also considered both divine and magical by many cultures.

How many golden ratio relationship triangles can you find in the regular pentagon with the inscribed pentagram? Pentagonal symmetry, or "symmetry of life," is found everywhere.

ANSWER: PAGE 123

If you take the principles of the golden section and apply them to two dimensions, you will arrive at the golden rectangle, into which you can inscribe a golden spiral (see below). Can you recognize that natural spiral on page 76?

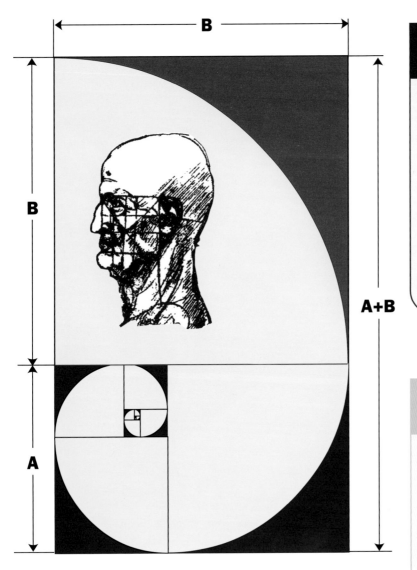

GOLDEN RECTANGLE
Dynamic symmetry in a face

In what is probably a self-portrait, Leonardo da Vinci has overlaid the picture with a square subdivided into rectangles, some of which approximate to golden rectangles. Leonardo was fascinated with golden proportions and the golden rectangle in, as he once described it, "geometrical recreations." He illustrated Luca Pacioli's book on the golden sections, called Divina Proportione *(Venice, 1509), and was fascinated by the human body and living shapes in general (witness his male nude—* The Vitruvian Man*).*

✳ Whirling spiral

The ancient Greeks discovered a special rectangle that has a unique property. Its two sides bear the "divine relationship," or the golden ratio, to one another. If you cut off the square B x B (see box, left), then the remaining rectangle has the same proportions as the original one. If we draw a quarter circle in each square of the subdivision of the golden rectangle we shall get a good approximation of the logarithmic spiral as shown.

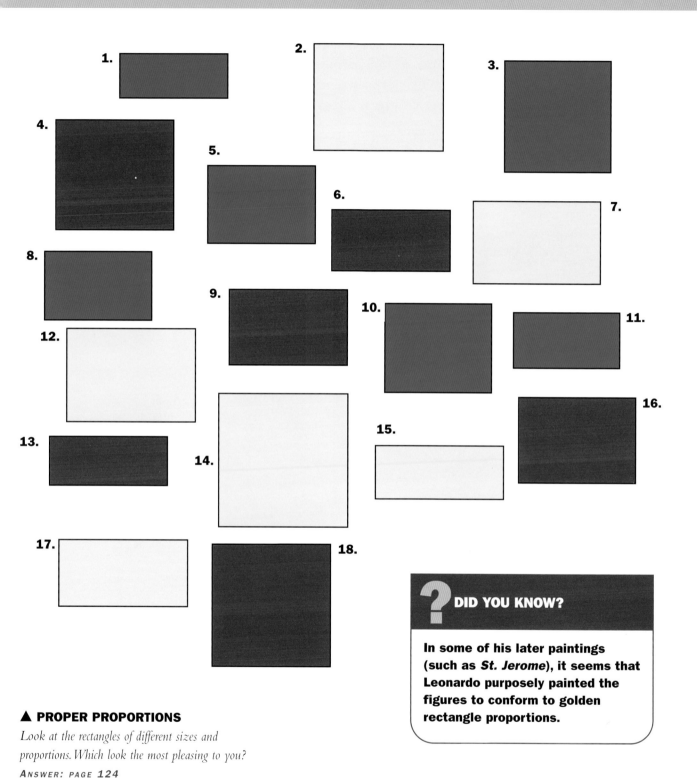

1.

2.

3.

4.

5.

6.

7.

8.

9.

10.

11.

12.

13.

14.

15.

16.

17.

18.

▲ PROPER PROPORTIONS

Look at the rectangles of different sizes and proportions. Which look the most pleasing to you?

ANSWER: PAGE 124

? DID YOU KNOW?

In some of his later paintings (such as *St. Jerome*), it seems that Leonardo purposely painted the figures to conform to golden rectangle proportions.

Racetrack is one of the most beautiful paper-and-pencil games ever devised. It is a convincing proof that simple games requiring only a sheet of paper and a pen can be as sophisticated and rewarding as any other.

▶ RACETRACK

Racetrack is a car-racing simulation game for several players and is played on graph paper. Based on an ingenious game principle, its origin is unknown, though it was first described by Martin Gardner in his Scientific American *recreational mathematics column.*

Racetracks should be made as curved as possible to make the race more interesting when played out. This will be made obvious by studying the sample game.

Each player has a pen of a different color as shown at the start line. At each turn a player moves his or her car forward to a new grid intersection point, according to these simple rules:

1. The new grid point and the straight line segment joining it to the preceding point must lie entirely within the track.

2. No two cars may simultaneously occupy the same point.

Acceleration and deceleration are simulated in the following ingenious way:

Assume that your previous move was "x" (straight forward) and "y" (left or right) units. The absolute difference between your straight move must be either 0 or 1, and the same for your left or right move. This means that a car can maintain its current speed or vary it by one unit distance per move. The first move according to this rule is one unit left or right, or forward, or both. A car that leaves the track loses two turns. The first car to cross the finish line wins.

▼ SAMPLE GAME

In the sample game below, blue slows too late to make the first turn efficiently. He narrowly avoids a crash. He takes the last curve superbly, however, and wins the race.

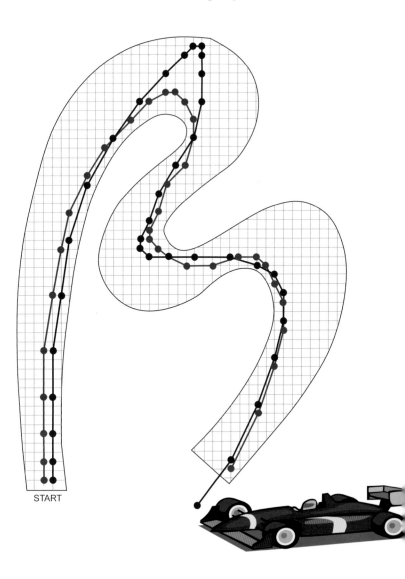

START

▼ THE TRACK

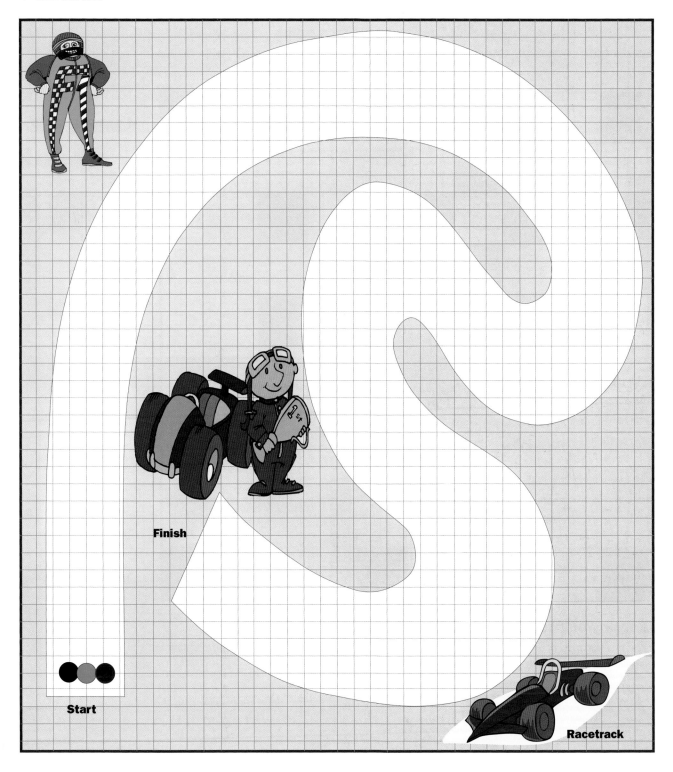

Finish

Start

Racetrack

This puzzle uses similar principles to two inventions: the pinhole camera and the camera obscura. The latter was a dark room with one small hole through which the outside image passed, allowing artists to trace scenes accurately, as if using an overhead projector.

▼ PEEPHOLES

What will you perceive looking through these four peepholes?

PEEPHOLE 1 *A flat painted hexagonal pattern.*

PEEPHOLE 2 *An interior concave corner of a cube.*

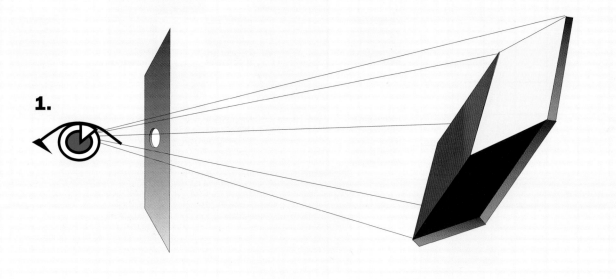

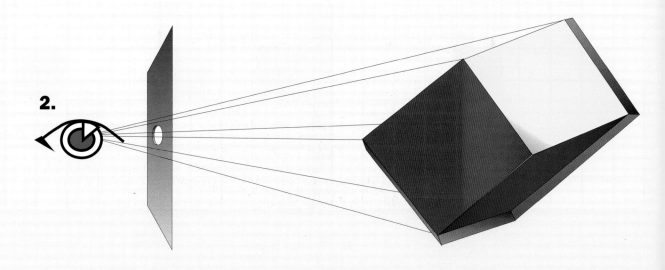

PEEPHOLE 3 *A three-dimensional cube*

PEEPHOLE 4 *A box with its interior painted.*

ANSWER: PAGE 124

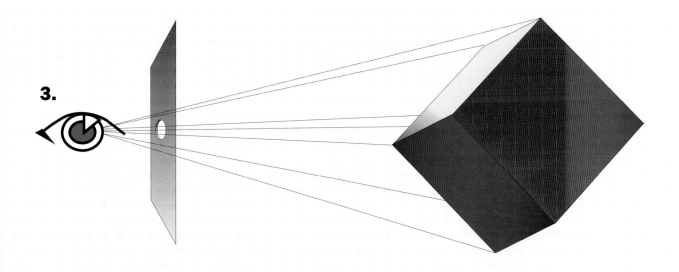

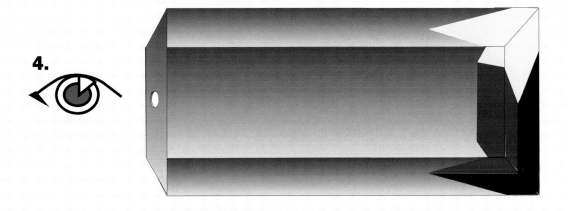

If you enjoy dot-to-dot puzzles you should enjoy these (though these will need a bit more thought). Each one offers an opportunity for a colorful journey.

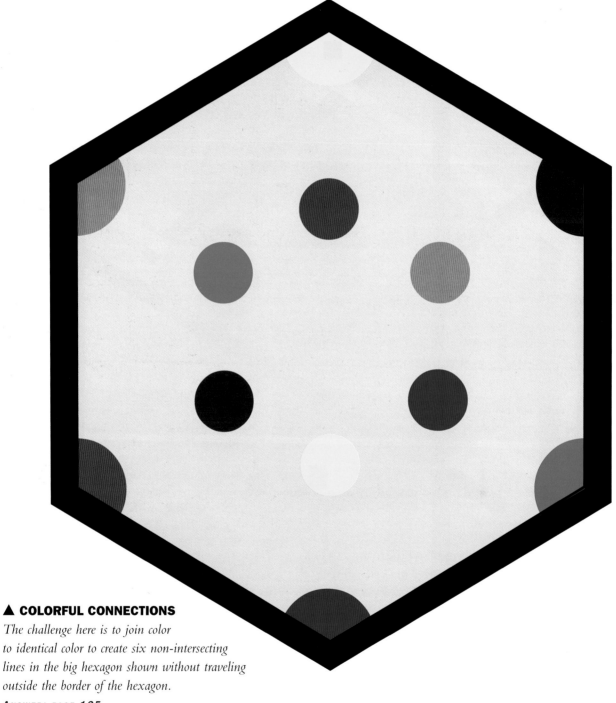

▲ COLORFUL CONNECTIONS

The challenge here is to join color to identical color to create six non-intersecting lines in the big hexagon shown without traveling outside the border of the hexagon.

ANSWER: PAGE 125

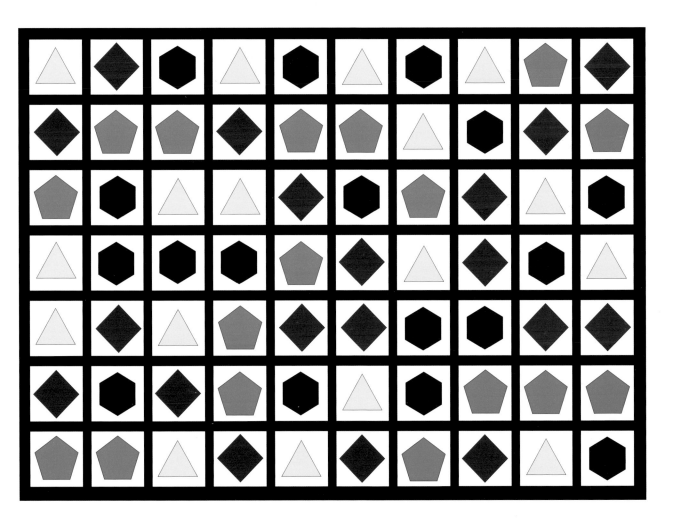

▲ SHAPELY STEPPING STONES

Can you find a route starting at the upper left box and traveling to the lower right box? You may move from box to box up, down, left, right, and diagonally, but only in the following sequence: triangle–square–pentagon–hexagon (yellow–red–green–blue).

ANSWER: PAGE **125**

The word "mosaic" comes from the Latin for "muse", from the decorations of medieval shrines dedicated to the Muses. Your task here is to identify regular shapes in a mosaic we've built, then try putting one together yourself.

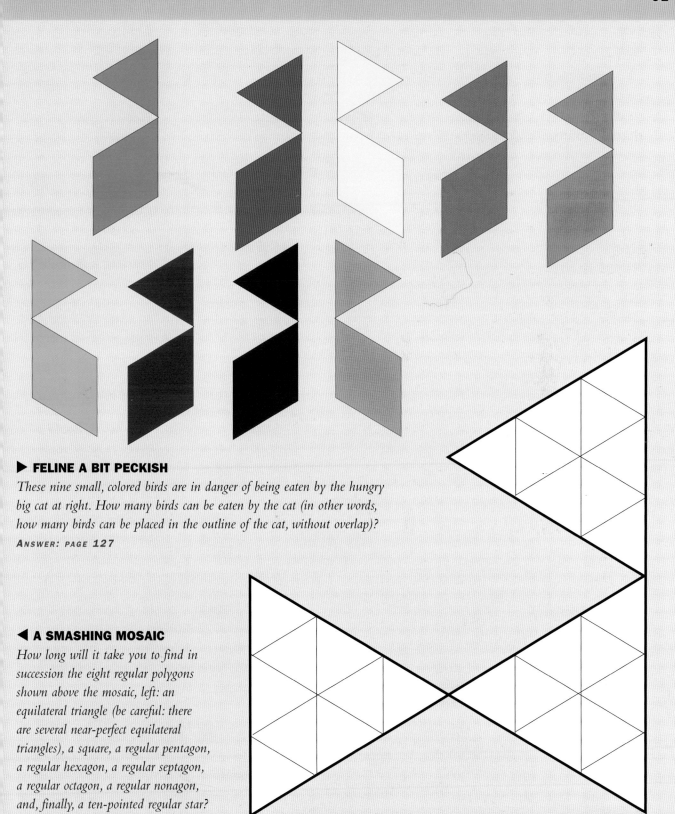

▶ FELINE A BIT PECKISH

These nine small, colored birds are in danger of being eaten by the hungry big cat at right. How many birds can be eaten by the cat (in other words, how many birds can be placed in the outline of the cat, without overlap)?

ANSWER: PAGE 127

◀ A SMASHING MOSAIC

How long will it take you to find in succession the eight regular polygons shown above the mosaic, left: an equilateral triangle (be careful: there are several near-perfect equilateral triangles), a square, a regular pentagon, a regular hexagon, a regular septagon, a regular octagon, a regular nonagon, and, finally, a ten-pointed regular star?

ANSWER: PAGE 126

Thinkline is one of a series of path-crossing games that can be played using the four types of pieces illustrated at right. The aim is to cross over the chasm, completing your path and preventing your opponent from completing his or hers! Once you've played this game, try using the same pieces to make up your own games for extra brain work.

▼ SAMPLE GAME

In this sample game, neither player wins. Both red and blue are missing just one piece to win the game.

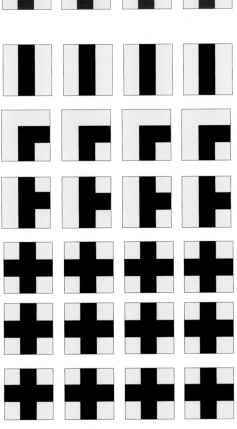

▲ THINKLINE
A PUZZLE GAME FOR TWO PLAYERS

Copy and cut out the 48 square tiles on the right of page 92 (or make a color copy of the page to cut out).

The pieces are mixed and placed in two stacks facing down. Each player has his or her own stack from which to pick. Players alternate moves by placing a tile adjacent to a tile already placed on the gameboard above. The object of

both players is to create a continuous line joining the two opposite sides of the gameboard.

As a solitaire puzzle problem using one player's pieces only, what is the shortest path to connect the two sides? The longest?

ANSWER: PAGE 127

Research shows that doing a puzzle a day boosts your self-esteem. So, before we bid you farewell, here are a couple of final opportunities to gain a well-deserved ego boost.

▲ CHECKS, MATE

Two players alternate coloring a square in a chessboard in either of two colors. The player forced to complete a solid color 2-by-2 square loses. Do you think one of the players can always force a win?

ANSWER: PAGE **128**

▼ FAR-TRAVELED

Can you choose any of the cities below, then make an all-inclusive round trip? The aim is to visit all the cities then return to the city from which you started, always following the directions indicated by the arrows on each line and never retracing the lines. For example, what will be the order of the round trip from New York and back visiting all the cities?

ANSWER: PAGE 128

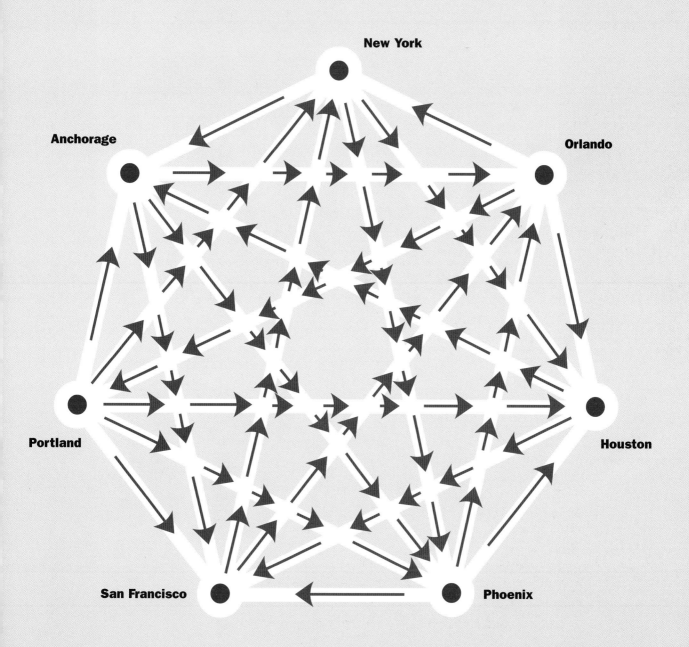

▶ THE HINGED SQUARE (page 6)

The answer is an equilateral triangle.

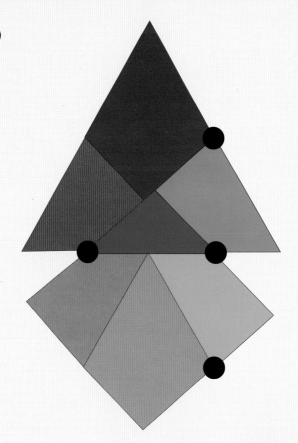

MIQUEL'S THEOREM (page 7)

This will always happen no matter where the points are placed.

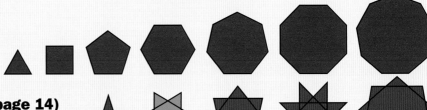

▶ REGULAR POLYGONS (page 14)

Stars (blue) and compounds (green) of the first seven regular polygons are shown. In general, these polygons are formed by marking p points around a circle then drawing lines between every q points.

For a regular polygon (red), q = 1. In other words, we draw a line between every consecutive point.

For a star polygon (blue), p and q are co-prime. That is, they share no common factors (other than 1), such as 2 and 5.

For a compound polygon (green), p and q share a common factor, such as 3 and 9.

▶ CIRCLE LOTTO (page 21)

The circles have to be fitted in the empty space matching the colors on the lotto card. Einstein's advice is:

"EVERYTHING SHOULD BE MADE AS SIMPLE AS POSSIBLE, BUT NOT SIMPLER —ALBERT EINSTEIN"

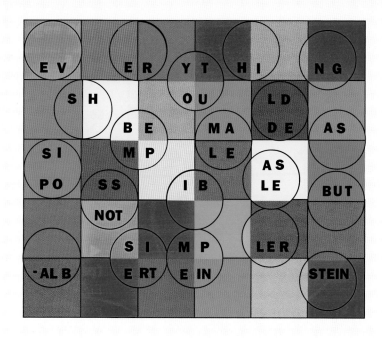

◀ BEELINE TO THE QUEEN (page 22)

The colors for each honeycomb indicate the number of touching cells for each. The pink honeycomb touches five adjacent cells.

In the honeycomb colony the only honeycomb touching five cells is the one shown—that of the queen bee.

▼ TRIANGULAR TRANSPORTERS (pages 28–29)

The correct curve is shown on each linkage and indicated in brackets beside it.

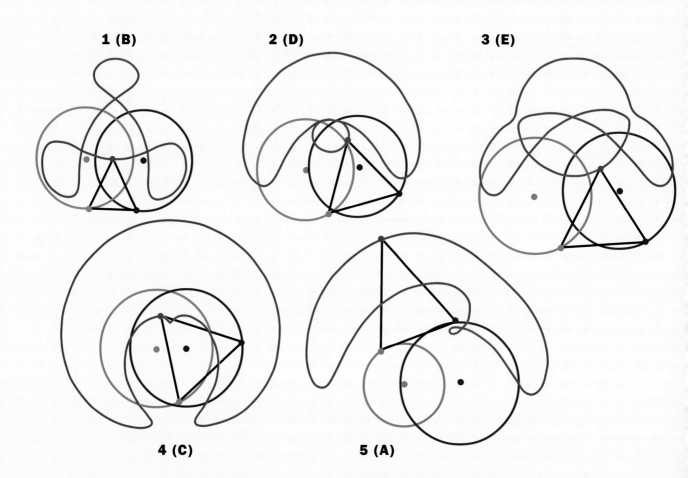

1 (B)   2 (D)   3 (E)

4 (C)   5 (A)

▼ THE NIGHTMARE BARCODE (page 31)

There is an odd element in the pattern, an orthogonal solid black unit square, which cannot be created from the given four elements.

Can you find it? (It appears 7 lines from the left and 17 lines up from the bottom.)

▶ COOL BODIES (page 32)

Sally has indeed received statues in three different sizes, but she's actually taken delivery of two large statues, one medium one, and a small one (instead of one large, two medium, and one small).

Without the confusing perspective of the wall behind the statues, this is what the statues would look like in the same order as given in the question:

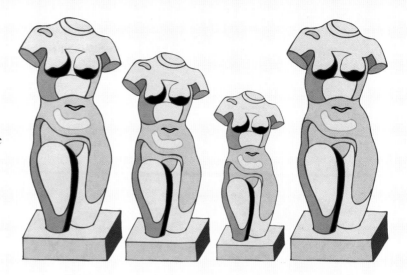

SIZE MATTERS (page 33)

The two sculptures are absolutely identical, believe it or not.

The cut

◀ DUDENEY'S QUILT (page 37)

This is one of the classic puzzles of Henry Dudeney, from 1931. An endless number of original variations of the problem followed.

The new quilt

▶ ON THE GARDEN PATH?
(page 40)

A simple closed curve (a bent or curved line) is one that does not cross itself. If you imagined it as a loop of string you could always rearrange it as a circle. Such a line divides the plane into two regions: an inside and an outside. How can you tell whether points in a simple closed curve are inside or outside?

One time-consuming way would be to trace or shade everywhere the point can get to without crossing any line. But there is a much more elegant and shorter way of finding out whether a point is inside or outside a simple closed curve. Draw a straight line from a point in question to the outside of the curve, and then count the number of times the straight line crosses the curve. If it crosses the curve an even number of times, the point is outside; if an odd number of times, it is inside. This rule is the famous "Jordan Curve theorem" of mathematics.

This rule works in our problem as well even if some parts of the closed curve are hidden. All inside regions are separated from each other by an even number of lines and any inside region is separated from any outside region by an odd number of lines. All cats are outside and only one mouse can be caught, shown by the arrow. The arrow crosses four fences—an even number—so we know it can be caught even though we can't see all of the maze.

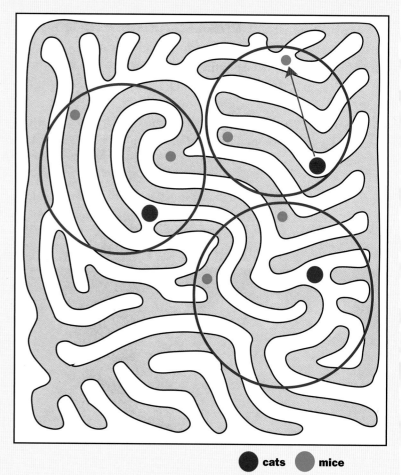

● cats ● mice

▶ INTERGALACTIC COMBAT (page 41)

One of the many possible configurations of the 40 starships is shown. No ship of any color is under attack by another ship of the same color.

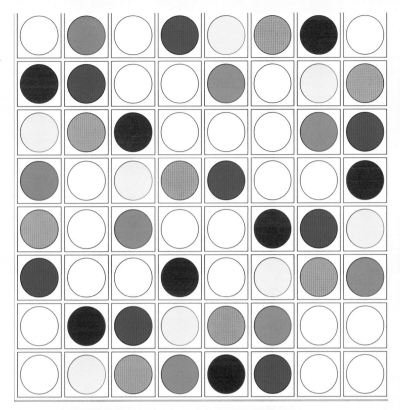

▶ ANT FILE (page 42)

Each circular element of the maze is rotated 90 degrees to create a continuous path through the aze from one part of the field to another.

▼ LADYBUG IN HIDING (page 43)

The leaves can be considered as nodes (points) of a graph. If a leaf has an even number of boundary crossings (overlaps with other leaves), the ladybug can enter and leave it, whereas a leaf with an odd number of boundary crossings can be entered and left by the ladybug but, when it finally reenters, it cannot leave again.

Observing the leaves, the only leaf with an odd number of crossings is the leaf under which the ladybug ends its journey and hides. Drawing a line through all the leaves that have only two crossings, and

marking the multiple crossed leaves, you can easily complete a continuous lines through all of the leaves, never retracing the line.

In general, a maze like this can be traversed if only 0 or 2 of the leaves have an odd number of adjacent leaves. If it's "0," you can start anywhere because it's a closed loop. If it's "2," those two leaves are the start and finish points. That's what we have in this case—the start point has one adjacent leaf, and the finish point has three adjacent leaves. All the others have even numbers of adjacent leaves.

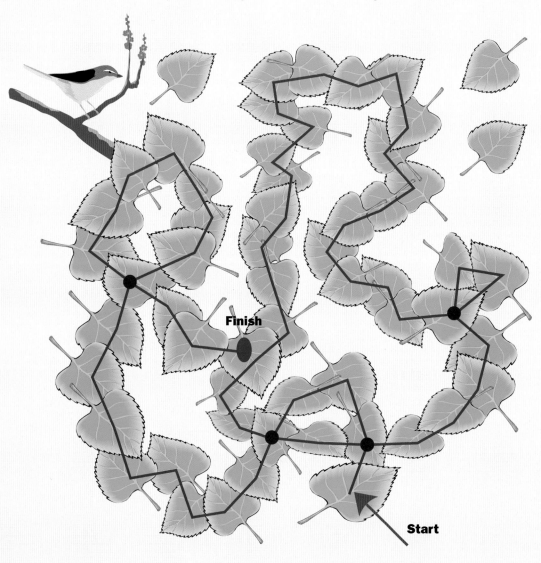

Finish

Start

▼ I-SPY (page 44)

The illegal alien spaceship entered from the top left planet and intended to leave from the lowest planet on the right, where it was intercepted by the waiting defense forces.

In the given graph, there are only two points with an odd number of edges. It can only be traced without crossing a route more than once if one of these points is the beginning or the end. We know that the upper point is the entry and so the lower point is the only possible end of the route, or the potential exit point.

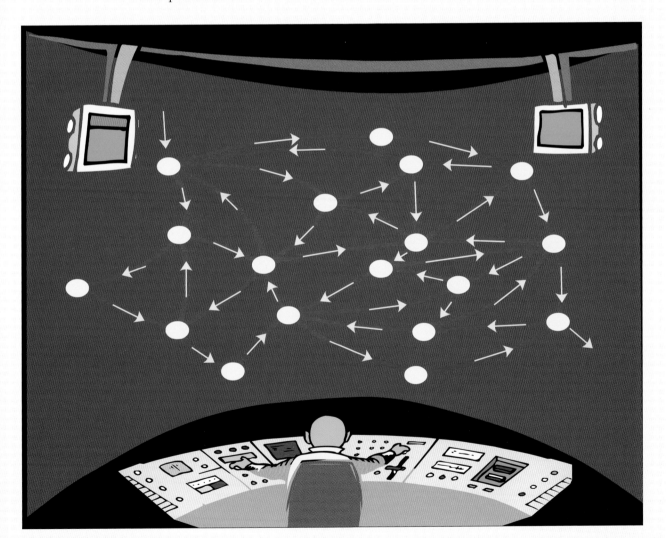

▼ FLEET ADMIRAL (page 45)

The sequence color code to lead the space fleet to land back home is:

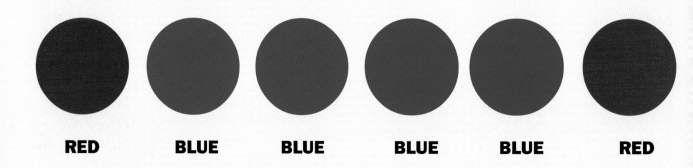

RED   BLUE   BLUE   BLUE   BLUE   RED

Observing the plan of the arrows reveals that it consists of five separate symmetrically oriented pentagons with four ships at their corners and the home planet at the fifth corner where they have to be led by the secret code. So it is enough to solve the route for one pentagon to solve the whole puzzle.

▼ LOST IN SPACE (page 46)

There are many ways the space station can be traversed according to the rules; one is shown.

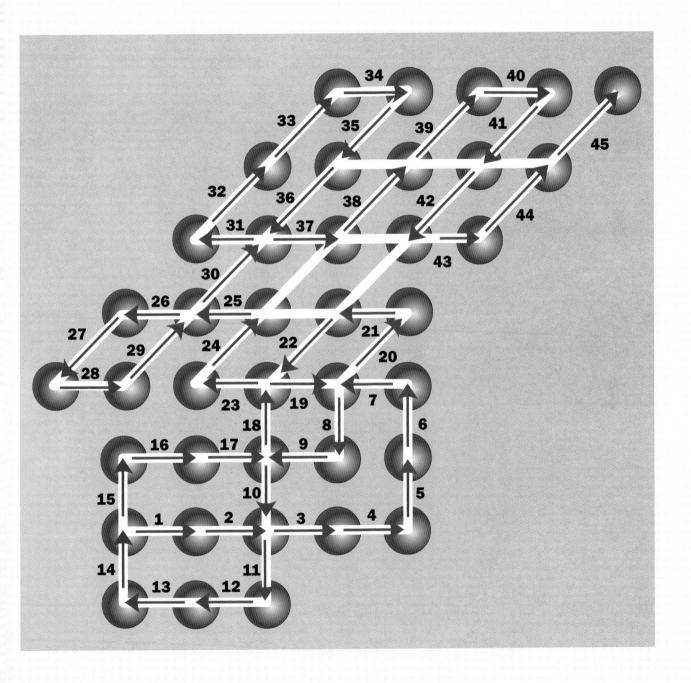

▼ SCHLEGEL'S SHORTCUT (page 47)

One possible solution to the problem is shown here on the
Schlegel diagram.

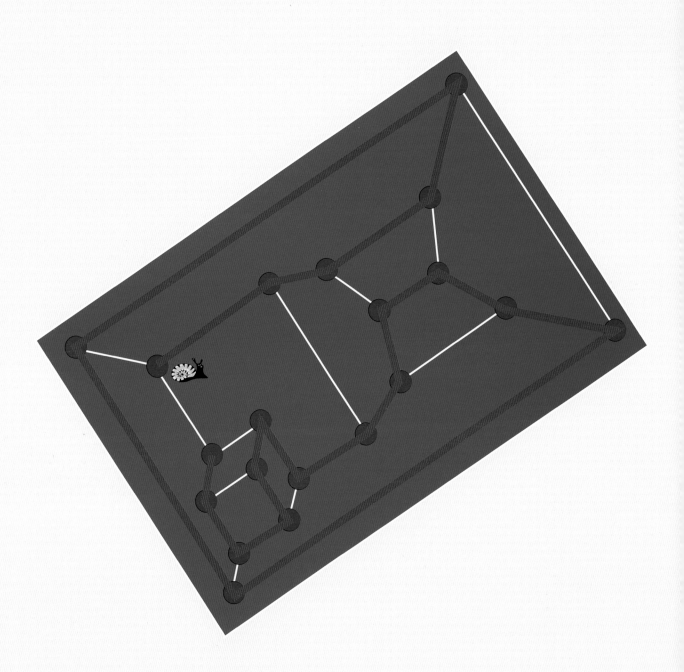

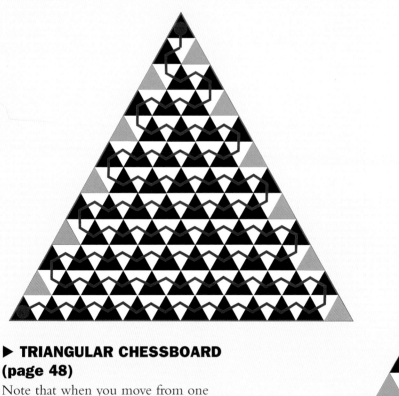

▶ TRIANGULAR CHESSBOARD (page 48)

Note that when you move from one triangle to the next, the color always alternates white to black to white and so on. Therefore, if there were (say) 40 white triangles, the highest number of black triangles we could possibly visit is 41 (by starting and ending on a black triangle).

If we count the triangles in the actual diagram, we find that there are 66 white triangles and 78 black triangles. We now know that the highest number of black triangles we can theoretically visit is 67, so therefore there will be at least 78 − 67 = 11 black triangles to which we cannot travel (shown in gray).

There are many ways of doing this, and two possibilities are shown here. By the previous calculation, however, we know that a better solution cannot be found.

LINEUP (page 49)

1 – 17	8 – 5	15 – 2	22 – 23
2 – 14	9 – 4	16 – 20	23 – 22
3 – 3	10 – 8	17 – 25	24 – 12
4 – 24	11 – 13	18 – 16	25 – 6
5 – 15	12 – 1	19 – 19	
6 – 18	13 – 10	20 – 21	
7 – 7	14 – 11	21 – 9	

▶ **GLOBE-TROTTING**
(page 52)

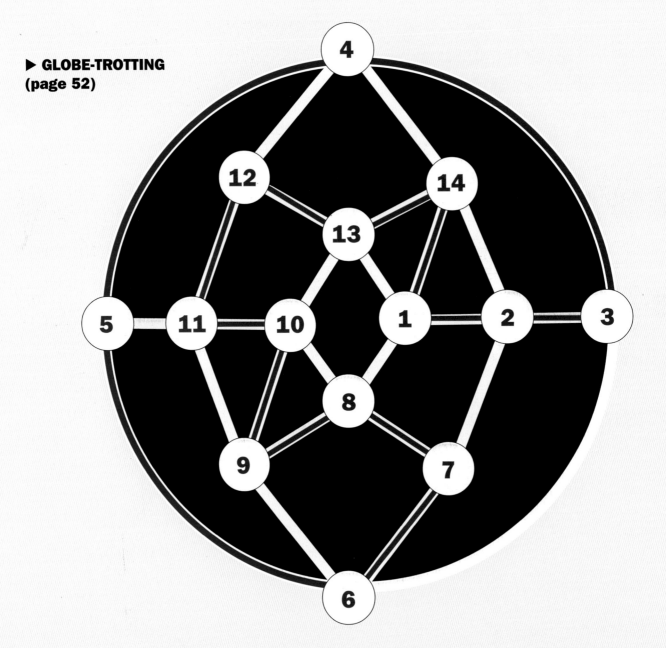

▼ RIGHT TO THE EDGE (page 53)

Three colors are sufficient, as one of the possible solutions
illustrated below shows.

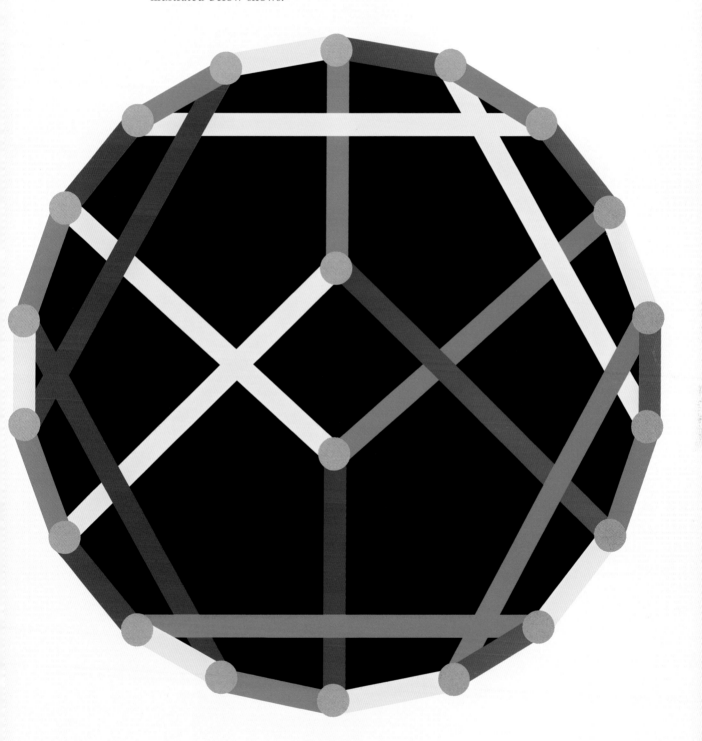

▼ **HOOP HOOP HOORAY! (page 54)**

Three colors are sufficient, as one of the possible solutions illustrated below shows.

▼ ROUNDABOUTS (page 55)

One solution is shown here.

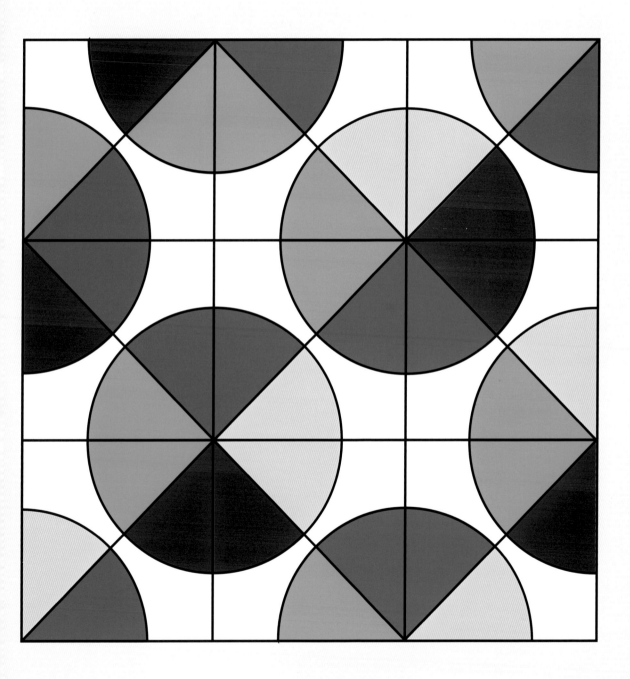

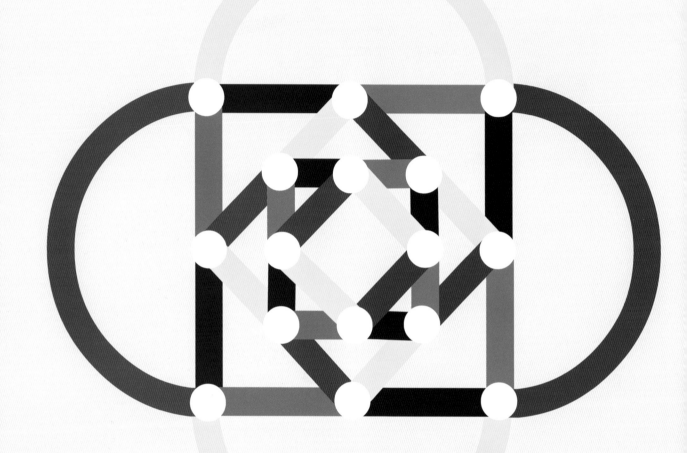

▲ PIPELINE PUZZLE (page 56)

You can color each line between two points using four colors,
so that there will be four different colors meeting at each point as
shown above.

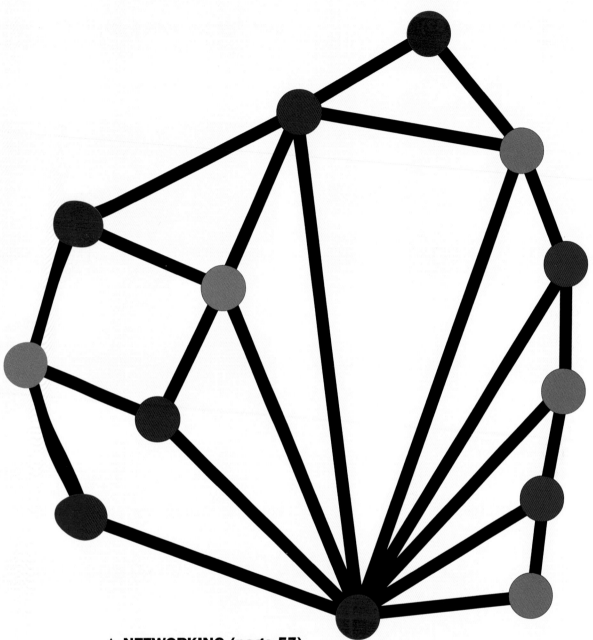

▲ NETWORKING (page 57)

Follow this method for vertex coloring:

1. Assign color 1 to the vertex of the highest degree (that is, the most lines meet in it).
2. Assign color 2 to the next highest degree vertex.
3. Find a vertex that forms the point of a triangle to the two points already colored, and assign it the unused color.
4. Follow on in this manner until all vertices are colored. According to these rules, the graph needs three colors, as shown.

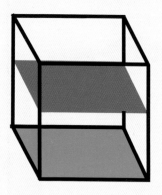
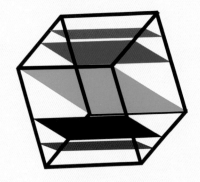
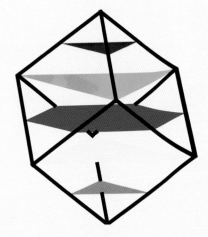

▲ CHEESE, PLEASE
(pages 94–95)

Imagine all three cubes of cheese lie on a horizontal table. In the first cube, you will always obtain a square if you take a slice that's parallel to the table.

If you tilt up the cube by 45 degrees, so that only one edge touches the table, more shapes are possible. Depending on the height of the cut you take, the resulting slices will range from squat to tall rectangles.

Now tilt the cube again so that only one point of the cube touches the table and the diametrically opposite corner is vertically above it. This time, the first slices you take will mostly be triangles. However, nearer the middle you will obtain some hexagons and, at one point halfway up, the slice will be a perfectly regular hexagon.

(To see why, note that the lines are the same length because they all run from the middle of one side of the cube to the middle of another side. Hence, it's a regular hexagon.)

The two pentagons shown in the question are impossible to obtain.

CHECKS, MATE (page 96)

The second player can always win by a symmetric strategy. He or she imagines the board divided horizontally. Each move of the first player is repeated by the second player coloring a symmetrically positioned square in the other half. For example, if the top right square is colored by the first player, the second player colors the bottom right, etc.

FAR-TRAVELED (page 97)

You will always be able to make round trips. For example, a New York round trip may be: NEW YORK—PHOENIX—HOUSTON—ANCHORAGE—ORLANDO—PORTLAND—SAN FRANCISCO—NEW YORK.